CONTENTS

PREFACE

I drank and socialised with murderers, but I was in love with a man who was kind and caring and I didn't see hatred or anger in him at all. It may sound sad, unbelievable, but for a long time I found Johnny Adair and his friends very good people. They were ordinary, average, fun-loving, trustworthy and dedicated, except for the fact that they killed. On 6 September 1995, my heart broke. My lover Johnny Adair was jailed for 16 years for directing terrorism and I didn't want to carry on without him. His big mouth and unquenchable need to brag about his actions sealed his fate. The idiot took a deal against the advice of everyone. He served only five years before being released under the provisions of the Good Friday Agreement. I can still hear the thump of the judge's hammer as the courtroom turned into a blur. I screamed as loud as I could, 'I love you and I'll wait for you, Johnny.'

The day before, he had broken off our relationship, telling me to get on with my life. But I wasn't about to desert him; he was my world. To me he was like a child and I was his comfort zone. If I had walked off then, I wonder would my sanity have been saved. How could I have known that I would travel up and down to prisons for years trying for a baby in a drab empty room, that I would shoplift and rob so he could dress well, smuggle vodka in balloons in my knickers, anything to please him. During those years I was addicted to drugs, dropped to six and a half stone and ended up in a psychiatric unit, twice. But nothing prevented me from loving my man. No matter how many times I attempted to walk away, he would beg me, 'Please, Jackie, you're the only person in this world who understands me.'

The police must have had a huge party that day. A lot of people were delighted that one of Belfast's most dangerous killers was eventually cleared off the streets. No doubt the politicians believed it would help the peace process. I loved him in an obsessive yet dependable way. I cherished him to the extent that I let him destroy me completely. I was the real 'loyalist'. He had no idea how to be loyal to anyone—not even himself. I knew it would be his downfall one day. The very last day we were together, he asked me to work in a loyalist-run brothel. He expected me to sink as low as he had. I told him it was over between us, broke his nose and kicked him out of my house. It was a dull and painful end.

I wait for the phone call now telling me he's dead. That day will arrive, and when it does it will be me who will visit his graveside, not his wife Gina. Johnny still hasn't learnt his lesson; he will continue to egg people on to 'come and get me', to prove the point that he remains vitally important, if not indispensable. He will not back off or get on with a normal life. He wants everyone to carry on acknowledging the 'Mad Dog' façade. He cannot accept that he is a has-been or that his time has simply passed. He needs to go out with a bang.

The Ulster Defence Association (UDA) that he belonged to bears a Latin slogan that for me is ironic—'*Quis Separabit*' meaning, 'Who will come between us?' His partner Gina personified that motto. Her merciless mind games ruined any chance we had of a normal relationship. Slowly but surely, in those early days of drinking and partying in loyalist drinking dens, I realised when people crowded around the 'wee man', that my lover, my new-found chance at life, was more than just a cheeky daredevil in a leather waistcoat and a baseball cap. He was a major player in a treacherous political game and pretty soon he would be guaranteed a place in history. Although Johnny and I were destined to be apart in the end, in many ways we were both prisoners of that same past. Neither of us can truly move on in our separate stories. It is as if history's roots are pulling us down. To this day I have no idea why it all happened, except that I feel it is time to tell my side of the story.

I desperately need to apologise to my son and daughter for the life I led them into at the time this story was lived. The emotional stress I must have put them through is indefensible. For my 16-year-old daughter, who had to bathe me when I was having a nervous breakdown, that was unbearably tough. As it was for my son, who was at the time so young and impressionable. I hope I can make it up to them. They both know how much I truly love them. I am going to be the best mother possible, now and in the future. They are my entire life; nothing else matters.

Finally, and most importantly, this book is dedicated to my beautiful sister Kim who died tragically in 2005. She lived in Belfast during the madness of the Adair years and helped me laugh my way through many difficult times. I miss her so much and am haunted by her loss.

Jackie 'Legs' Robinson 2006

ACKNOWLEDGMENTS

Special thanks are extended to the following who helped and co-operated with completion of Jackie's story: Henry McDonald, Neil Ward, Louise Browne, Kelvin Boyes, Jim McDonald, Trish Gray, Charla and Billy Robinson, Jean Kiddell, Billy and Ann McKelvie, Isabel Jackson, Karen McDowell, Angela McDonald.

01 | WIVES AND OTHER WOMEN

He gave me a new lease of life and then he set out to destroy it. If I had known just how much he would break my heart, I would have sent the wee fat bastard packing. Yet I have to admit that I did truly love him. And I'll visit his graveside long after he's gone because there's only one possible homecoming for Johnny Adair.

If you're going to have an affair with a terrorist and drink in the same bar as his wife, it helps to be immune to fear. In the Diamond Jubilee Bar on the Shankhill Road, Belfast, early in 1992, Paddy Patterson, a then senior member of the UDA's C Company, took Jackie Robinson aside and advised her to make a quick exit. Johnny Adair's long-term partner Gina had just arrived and was tipped off that Adair's new love interest was enjoying a night out with friends and wasn't too pushed about moving. Although Johnny was constantly having affairs, this time it seemed different. He was 'coming back for more', and close friends realised he was besotted. The immediate bellyache, however, was Gina, who didn't take kindly to legitimate love rivals. While it was probable that everyone knew about both women, up until now they had never been in the same room together.

Patterson's warning had to be seen in the context of the premises Jackie Robinson was drinking in. The Diamond Jubilee had a notorious reputation as a loyalist drinking den from the start of Ulster's Troubles. Several men, both loyalists and Catholics, had been kidnapped, taken to the bar, and interrogated under torture before being dragged away for a kneecapping, or worse still, a savage beating or death.

Sexual one-upmanship and power play-offs were typical of how a serious political campaign explosively collided with primitive hormonal warfare throughout the tail end of the Troubles in Belfast. The quirk of fate on this night would reveal itself three years later, leaving Paul Orr, the UDA's welfare officer, beaten to pulp on blood-spattered waste ground in west Belfast, screaming for his life. Hypocritically, Adair's *modus operandi* regularly involved dishing out lethal beatings for any man who slept with his wife-to-be, Gina. He didn't tolerate infidelity towards him; it made him feel discarded and small.

'There was a lot of bed hopping going on throughout the political struggle,' says Jackie. 'Affairs were happening all over the place in betweeen the murder and the mayhem. Justice was achieved through violence. While people felt comfortable judging me, their own husbands and wives were also playing the field big time. It was just part of life; you simply got used to it.

'Johnny told me Gina would be in the bar on this night, but up until then I had never seen her in person. "You know what to do," he told me. A few pals and myself had gone out for a drink as normal and I certainly wasn't out to cause trouble. I couldn't believe it when I saw the infamous Gina Crossan. She was dreadfully manly looking—not at all what I expected. There was nothing feminine or sexy about her; she was very butch with a mop of peroxide, and her dress sense was atrocious. I had heard rumours that she was a hard nut, nifty with an AK-47 in her hands and all that, but prancing around feeding off her partner's reputation didn't cut it with me. I wasn't afraid of her in the slightest.

'She kept staring over at our table, making it obvious that someone had told her about me. She probably thought she could intimidate me. She stood up, marched across the room, bent over our table very slowly and put her cigarette out, all the while staring at me. I laughed out loud. She mooched back over to

Johnny and started giving it lots in his ear. He was flinging his hands about, telling her to get lost. Again I was asked to leave, but I made it clear I wasn't going anywhere.

'I went to the loo after a while, not realising that Gina was in there. The door opened and she pushed her way past me with Paul Orr's wife, Elaine. Elaine had told Gina in the toilets, as I later found out, "Watch out for the blonde one", letting her know I was involved with Johnny. I later became good friends with Elaine. Yet that night when she told Gina about me, she had no idea that her own husband was sleeping with Gina. Three years later he would be severely beaten and left on waste ground on Johnny's orders. He was just one of at least a dozen men who were ruthlessly battered for sleeping with Gina.'

—

The new brood of 'graduates' who rose from commonplace street violence to the upper ranks of the UDA leadership in the early 1990s were not only steadfast defenders of the loyalist faith and militant killers, they were the sexual equivalent of a Venus flytrap, the plant that lures its prey using sweet-smelling nectar. The big boys of Ulster had their own brand of nectar—an appetite for violence and incessant partying—and women of all ages and backgrounds were becoming deliciously addicted. Furtive partner swapping, dirty dealings and covert sexual relationships with Catholic women—considered to be the enemies of Ulster—would become routine. Murder . . . Party . . . Sex . . . Politics barely shimmered in the background like a computer screensaver.

Adair originally grew to prominence following revelations in 1989 of collusion between loyalist paramilitaries and British security forces that ended the career of various long-standing UDA leaders. The power rupture created opportunism for other subordinate members to rise unexpectedly fast. The organisation had formed in 1972 with the merging of a number of local defence groups to guard loyalist communities against attacks by republican activists. Originally, the groups were autonomous, but within a few years a co-ordinated strategy emerged with various brigades, battalions and companies throughout each county and city in Ulster. C Company was always the UDA unit from the Lower Shankill since its inception in 1973. However, it did not come into its own as an operative terror squad until the UDA had been reorganised in north and west Belfast following the arrest of the old guard leadership over the collusion scandal. Ironically, C Company came to the fore due to the security forces' attempt to clean up their own act over the leaking of files on republican suspects to the UDA.

A welfare section, Loyalist Prisoners' Aid (LPA), also became part of its remit, as well as a military wing known as the Ulster Freedom Fighters (UFF). The UDA's main activities were community development, vigilante patrols, and of course the killing of key republican figures.

It was ironic that the very leaders young Adair and his cronies superseded in the late 1980s had forced a lot of young recruits into the Ulster Young Militants (UYM) in the first place. The wayward teenagers were hauled in for anti-social behaviour such as burglary and car theft, and were given the choice between joining up or taking metal in the knee (kneecapping). They chose the uncomplicated option, declining the offer of violence, and were schooled for 'wee jobs' by political figureheads charged with the task of policing dilapidated loyalist communities. The UYM was later described by a high-ranking police officer as 'Frankenstein's Monster' for the way it managed to slowly ingratiate young men into violence.

By the late 1980s Adair, a teenage skinhead and early school leaver, had become leader of the UFF in the Shankill Road district during some of the most violent years of terrorist activity. By the end of 1992 the UDA/UFF had outdone the IRA murder count for the first time ever.

—

'Gina knew Johnny had a lot of women before me, but she didn't like it if he kept going back to one particular woman,' says Jackie. 'That would insinuate involvement and she was a very jealous person. She referred to me as the "auld dog with the white hair and good figure". Exceptionally money-oriented, I don't think she gave a shit as long as he gave her what she wanted, a few hundred quid on the table at the end of every week. Having said that, she didn't want any prolonged humiliation either, which is what I turned out to be.

'So that night in early February 1992, it was all out. Gina knew within six weeks of me seeing Johnny, but it would be a long time before we would finally have it out with a punch-up in a traffic jam on Agnes Street in west Belfast. That same street today, in 2006, has graffiti that reads: "Adair—Loyalist Wife Beater". It goes to show how hard a fall even the important are destined to suffer.'

At the same time as the affair with Jackie (nicknamed Legs Robinson because of her fondness for short skirts) progressed, Adair was fast emerging as a hero, intent on lugging the war to the IRA's door, using a level of unprompted aggression rarely seen since the era of the Shankill Butchers in the 1970s. While the Butchers' idea of an enjoyable night out was to abduct any Catholic passer-by and leisurely torture him to death, Adair and his clique used drink and drugs as a springboard to sanction hit-and-miss violence. Their intended targets were republican activists, but the 'brief' often widened to include arbitrary members of the nationalist community and fallen loyalists who said or did anything out of place.

He rarely carried out any of the killings himself, preferring instead to act as C Company's mouthpiece, handing out orders and blindly consenting to kill any possible tout who interfered with the cause. What he lacked in charisma and intellect, he made up for in brawn. He had a well-developed sense of humour, was characteristically cheeky and partied like a lunatic on day release. His trademark waistcoat, baseball cap, trackies, gold jewellery, tattoos and white Reeboks became a distinctive off-duty uniform in the loyalist drinking dens of south and east Belfast. Addicted to high fashion, class A drugs, hardcore revelry and oodles of sex, his cronies could only admire him whilst women resorted to ridiculous measures to lure the merry muscle man into bed.

He was persistently more loyal to his libido than to the cause if he spotted a woman he liked. The more notorious he became in the 1990s for cranking up the UDA murder machine, the more succulent sexual favours he was served up on a plate. He is known to have had at least one illegitimate child from this period, in addition to four with Gina. He had at least three long-term affairs and several short tempestuous ones, such as the Cathy Spruce fiasco in 1991. That ended up with him being arrested and accused of terrorist activities after she peddled details of his goings on to the police. Jackie herself spent six years trying for a child with him, even inside the jail. She set a precedence at the Maze Prison in 1994 by being the first woman (not his wife) allowed by prison officers to have sex with a convicted terrorist in a specially allocated private space. It is something she still thinks about today.

'I was desperate to have a child with him, as any woman wishes for when she is truly in love,' she maintains. 'I know people are going to have a hard time understanding how someone could fall in love with the likes of Johnny Adair, but behind the combat façade was a soft-hearted fun man who was basically very lost. He was treasured by almost everyone at the time and he was addicted to the attention they gave him. He has a dire reputation now, sure, but I saw many sides to this man at the time. He was notoriously generous. People would literally fall over themselves to shake his hand as his popularity grew. Even being vaguely associated with him meant you had no chance to pay for your drinks. I don't think I bought one drink that entire time. He had champion status and got off on it to the point of being permanently on a high.

'Johnny noticed me straight away the first night I ventured into the Taughmonagh club with my cousin, but I thought he was just a wee fat bastard, to be honest. It was quite late on a Sunday night. I wore a short pink and black dress and my hair was tied up. This figure from nowhere descended on us. "What's her name? Tell her I want her," he said to my friend. I was a bit taken aback. I was embarrassed for him. I'm not one for thinking that I'm God's gift to anyone; the opposite, in fact. I'm very shy in social situations. He was wearing a pair of jeans, a short-sleeved shirt and leather waistcoat and a baseball cap. I looked at him in amazement and turned away. A commander from the estate shouted over, "Oi mate, the Queen is being played on the tele 'ere, do you mind?" It was so funny, this up-and-coming loyalist god ignoring the head of the royal family because he was more concerned with what was going on in his trousers. A lot of people at the time didn't recognise Johnny Adair for being much at all. He was only starting to be a "someone".

'I had only begun to go out again myself, venturing to the local drinking den in the estate where some of my relations lived. My marriage of 15 years had fallen apart in Birmingham, and I was raring to go for a new start. Looking back, I wasn't fully aware of how different I looked in such a short space of time. Within a matter of months I had gone from drab to, well, looking bloody good. My grey hair had turned white-blonde from stress, the long skirts shot up, and muscles appeared after working out for the first time in years. Men were staring a lot. I thought to myself, what the bloody hell are they looking at for God's sake? Are they just perverts? I didn't understand the change. It had been a long time since I looked and felt so good.'

Jackie moved from Northern Ireland to the UK and back again from the age of 13, but her heart was always firmly rooted in Belfast and she knew she would end up living there permanently. On 10 July 1957, Jacqueline White was born at 9 Monarch Street, south Belfast, and life in Northern Ireland was quiet, traditional, and like the rest of Ireland, relatively poor.

—

There was a type of insidious innocence sandwiched between the post-war years before the Troubles began. A lot of emphasis was placed on family life and earning a decent living in one of Belfast's many industries, including the linen mills and the infamous shipyard. Up until February 1957, for instance, the BBC and ITV had a broadcasting break between 6 and 7 p.m., known as the Gap, or Toddlers' Truce, to enable parents to get their children to bed. Life was, for the most part, improving. Many of the slum areas were being cleared and new housing estates (with modern amenities such as indoor toilets) began to dot the Belfast landscape. A post World War II Westminster Labour government introduced free secondary school education and working-class people also had the chance to attend university for the first time. By the early 1950s Northern Ireland had a fully formed welfare state and health service, the same as the rest of the UK.

A clear indication of what was important in Northern Ireland that year can be seen in the Acts of the Northern Ireland Parliament for 1957. The King George VI Memorial Youth Council Act (Northern Ireland) 1957 was introduced to ensure that parts of May Street in the city of Belfast would be used by the Council 'to encourage the development of body, mind and spirit through physical and cultural activities, and to inculcate qualities of leadership and, especially, to promote the well-being of young people through any form of physical or cultural activity'; while the Marketing of Eggs Act (Northern Ireland) 1957 saw to the provision of the packaging of eggs at markets and laid out strict criteria for preparations of liquid egg and the storage of pickled eggs!

Politically, of course, things were slightly more complicated than pickled eggs. On 1 January 1957 one of the most villainous incidents of the IRA's six-year border campaign took place. An attack on the police station in the small village of Brookeborough, Co. Fermanagh, resulted in the death of two members of the IRA, Fergus O'Hanlon and Sean South. South's funeral a few weeks later in his home city of Limerick attracted thousands of sympathisers. In response to the ongoing IRA border campaign, the authorities on both sides of the border decided to reintroduce internment.

A general election in the Republic of Ireland led to yet another change in government. The electorate decided to reject the coalition government and to return Éamon de Valera to office. One of the most noteworthy features of the result was the re-emergence of Sinn Féin (SF) with the party gaining its highest share of the vote for 30 years.

The re-emergence of radical armed republicanism after

decades of slumber didn't at first provoke any violent or panicked loyalist response. In the late 1950s Northern Ireland's position within the UK looked secure. The province had provided thousands of volunteers who had stuck by Britain in its darkest hour when the nation was isolated and under threat from Nazi invasion. A decade after the end of the war, Ulster was experiencing an economic upturn and, unlike their counterparts in the Republic, the people of the North were getting used to the welfare state set up by the Labour government in 1945. Protestant Ulster looked content and confident as it was about to enter a new decade, one which would eventually shake the Northern Ireland state to its foundations. But in the hiatus between the dourly conservative certainties of the 1950s and the turbulent 1960s, even the poorest sections of the Protestant community felt safe.

—

'Life was simple, but hard too,' says Jackie. 'Sometimes I think my life was destined to be bizarre. Even my early memories are eerie. I was baby-sitting for my mum's friend off the Donegall Road. The kid had a cleft palate. It was the first time I had seen anyone with something like that. We decided to hold a séance in the house. I was 8 years old. We got a table out, pulled the curtains shut and lit a fire. There were a few older fellas there, some friends and myself. We put the glass in the middle of the table with handwritten letters placed around in a circle. The glass started to move and I knew no one was pushing it. At one stage it lifted, flew up and smacked off the fireplace, and the table jumped up and banged down again. Everyone ran out of the house and left me on my own to look after the baby. I always felt my life changed from that day. I somehow managed to curse myself. Either that or I was simply so scared to death that I was never the same afterwards.

'There were a lot of weird elements in my early life. My dad used to hypnotise people for a laugh, using a scar on his nose. He would ask people to focus on the scar and they'd fall under hypnosis. One night, one of our young neighbours decided he'd let my dad hypnotise him. My dad was talking away and after about ten minutes the lad jumped up suddenly and started screaming like a mad man and ran out into our backyard. He had seen his dead brother who was killed during the war. He never visited us again after that.

'Monarch Street seemed like a really long strip of road when I was a kid. There was just myself, one older sister than me, one brother and three younger sisters. It was a fun place to grow up, but there was also a lot of sadness—a lot of fights at home. My mum worked at the Monarch Laundry, so we ran around the street after school where she could keep an eye on us. That's what it was like in those days; kids did their own thing. My dad was a lorry driver with Harkness. Giant lorries would take over the street and you could smell the dead cows and sheep. He was also a member of the Territorial Army (TA), so he was away a lot. We amused ourselves as best we could by making use of everything around us, even the weather. When it rained hard and the drains filled up, we would put on our swimming costumes and paddle away. At the top of the street was the Blackwater river; we called it the Blackie. It was mangy dirty and stuffed with rats. It was fascinating for us kids because it was also full of old bicycles and bed mattresses and all sorts of rubbish. We knew the rats were there somewhere, but it didn't stop us getting in and having a good look around.

'We always sat around in a small group at home when a baby was due. We would huddle in the back bedroom on the double bed waiting for the arrival of a new brother or sister. You would never hear a sound from my mum, not a screech. The first thing you'd hear would be the noise of a baby crying and you knew then there was a new family member. I remember Kim being born most of all. She died tragically in 2005. She had jet-black hair and the most beautiful olive skin. My mum always decorated the bedroom about a week before the baby's arrival. When the youngest was born, my brother and my other two sisters and myself sat in complete silence for hours on end with our heads in our hands waiting. My dad was standing at the door when we heard the baby cry. Terry wanted a brother and when the nurse announced it was another girl, Terry piped up, "I'm sick of this 'ere no more boys in this house. It's not on!" He stormed off. He was really pissed off, but he came around towards the end of the first week and bought the baby a bar of chocolate—I suppose to get rid of his guilt. It must have been hard for him being the only boy.

'A lot of the mothers were under a huge amount of stress in those days. Looking back, I think my mum suffered with post-natal depression. She seemed sad a lot when I was a kid. We got on so well; I love her so much. We're very close. But in those days women hadn't a chance to realise there was more to life than having babies and being there for the men. Mum did try to have a social life of her own. She went out quite a bit. I used to sit and listen at the top of the stairs when she'd bring friends back, pulling my vest around my knees, waiting for her. I'd fall asleep and fall down the stairs. I used to believe that when you closed the front door, the whole world stopped; nothing else happened outside our home. I suppose I felt a bit disoriented at a certain age. I used to think when my cousin Ann came to visit, if she didn't stay and play for as long as I wanted, I'd have to hit her with the poker. I did that in a rage one time when she tried to leave and I split her head open. I didn't want her to go, but after that it sure as hell meant she didn't come back again. I was lonely because I had a lot of responsibility put on me looking after the other kids.

'My routine was to get up early and take the two younger ones to the childminder, Mrs Winters, in Donegall Pass. I'd get ready then and go to school. When I came home, I'd do the housework, go to the butcher's shop and get food ready for mum to make the dinner. I was well known on the road for bartering with the butcher, Mr Skellington. "That's too dear Mr for that lump there. I'll tell me ma on ye." I was made aware from a young age that the world was a harsh place and you had to negotiate your way through it.

'When I think of family life now, it's so much more routine, so protected. Back then, a lot of people came and went through our house doing their own thing, like a lot of homes. Big fat George used to come in and sit on the settee. When my dad was out on a

Saturday night, he would call one of my sisters down and say, "Give us a wank." He was a friend of my cousin who was later charged with murder. His dick was shrivelled up like a snail. I remember walking in at the age of 9 and seeing it just lying there like a rotting sausage. "You better put that away or I'll tell my dad on you," I roared. You had every type of character wandering in and out, from holy to bad to deviant.

'There was a lot of so-called low-level abuse around. It was a time when adults knew children wouldn't dare speak up. People don't really talk about it now. I was also abused later on by a boy who lived near by, a friend of my dad. He was only about 17 years old. He had black curly hair and he was intensely angry looking all the time. He would come upstairs, pull my knickers down and start messing about. I was about 10 years old. He'd say to me, "If you don't do this, God will strike you down." I knew it was wrong, but I was very afraid; he would buy me sweets afterwards. He lives in that area to this day. He's married now with a couple of kids. I often wondered what he was like with his own youngsters. Life was crazy back then, and of course it got even crazier with the Troubles. Every nut in the packet had another reason to get angry.'

On the brink of the Troubles in 1967, an incident occurred that involved one of Jackie's relatives who also lived on Monarch Street. A cousin who liked to dig up graves, kill animals and tinker about with devil worship, slaughtered a woman and dumped her body in a dustbin. 'We didn't find out for a decade who was responsible,' says Jackie. 'It was a brutal attack and very rare in Belfast at that time. The woman's breast had been cut off and shoved in her mouth. She had been raped and suffered multiple stabbings. It was dreadful because she was considered a bit 'slow' and used to wander up the Falls Road talking to anyone and everyone despite being warned of the potential danger. On her way back one evening, my cousin and another man stopped her, dragged her down a laneway and began assaulting her. It turned out that she recognised them and said she was going to report them. Well, that sealed her fate.

'At first it was assumed someone from the Falls Road had done it, but they were two local men known to her. Although there was a massive hunt for the murderers, the crime wasn't solved until the late 1970s. This cousin of mine was a barman in Taughmonagh and bragged about how he'd committed the murder. He was eventually put away for it.

'Life at home bobbed along at the usual pace. I often lay in bed at night listening to my mum and dad fighting in the next room, waiting for the two of them to get stuck in. If it sounded really heavy, I would run in and get in between the two of them. They behaved strangely towards each other at times; it was very up and down. For instance, one Christmas my dad crashed his motorbike on the West Link towards Lisburn; the land around it was a meadow with cows and bulrushes and frogs and all kinds of stuff. My mum was peeling spuds in the kitchen when he walked in covered in blood. My mum ran at him with a knife shouting, "You fucking bastard, you've ruined our Christmas Day." She was left on her own to cope with a lot and I don't think that kind of "automatic parenthood" suited everyone.'

Like most people born in the late 1950s, Jackie vividly remembers when President Kennedy was shot in November 1963 and when Armstrong and Aldrin landed on the Moon in July 1969 but, remarkably, she can't pinpoint exactly when the Troubles began. On a lot of Belfast streets, Catholics and Protestants lived harmoniously together. 'It's hard to pinpoint for a child,' asserts Jackie. 'Sometime in 1968, I was told one day not to call around to the Neasons. They were leaving the neighbourhood in a hurry. I wasn't allowed to play with them any more. I ran around as fast as I could. They were packing up their things. My friend's mum said to me, "She's not allowed to play with you any more," pointing to her daughter. She seemed really angry. When my dad came and got me I asked him why they were going off like that all of a sudden, but nothing was properly explained. He said that one day it would be clear, but for the time being all I needed to know was that it was happening, that's all. More and more Catholic families started moving out of my area after that.'

—

Loyalists look upon the late 1950s as a lost idyll, suffering as many of them do from selective memory syndrome. Many still to this day cannot accept that beneath the surface of normality and increasing prosperity post-war Northern Ireland was founded on structural discrimination against its Catholic/nationalist minority. Ironically, the very reforms in 1945 that some unionists believed would win increasing numbers of Catholics to the cause of the union created a new generation of young radicals determined to challenge the status quo. They included Bernadette Devlin, a Queen's University graduate from Co. Tyrone, whose opposition to the unionist regime at Stormont eventually made her into a world renowned radical. Dubbed by the British press a 'mini-skirted Castro', Devlin's mixture of new left Marxism and traditional nationalist antipathy towards the unionist government turned her into the darling of the nascent Northern Ireland Civil Rights movement. Elected one of the youngest MPs in British history, Devlin personified that generation of young Catholics who took advantage of the British welfare state's free education. To many unionists, especially the poor and uneducated Protestant lower class, she represented a threat to their state.

—

Jackie Robinson's memory of anti-Devlin propaganda at the start of the Troubles illustrates the mistrust and exaggerated sense of fear the unionist ruling elite engendered in their own people. 'I remember people on the street saying she had thrown stones at Unity flats and all hell broke loose after that, but in reality it was just misinformation. In my child's memory, however, it marked the beginning of the Troubles. Dads went out in the evenings without explanation; mums stayed at home looking desperately worried. My dad would say to my mum, "Mind the kids" and off he'd go. Then the soldiers came to Northern Ireland. We were taken to stay at a friend's house in Donegall Gardens. They tucked us up in the back room and the woman in the house stayed and looked after us.

'Terry and myself used to go up to the mountains at the top of the Whiterock Road. We would walk around looking at different graves. When a riot broke out between Catholics and Protestants after the soldiers arrived, some Catholic friends got word that we were playing there, came looking for us and brought us back safely to our dad. That was probably the last time we were helped by Catholics. We were afraid to go out after that. Barbed wire and barricades filled the streets and life seemed to change overnight.

'At first the soldiers were a real novelty. They would kneel down until their eyes were on our level, chatting away. We'd ask them if we could have a look at their guns and they'd show us, satisfying our curiosity. You see, even they didn't realise the seriousness of the situation or how hazardous it had become. The women would come out and make them tea. The Catholic women did that for a while too. When the Troubles started the soldiers were well received by the nationalist community. Their presence made everyone feel safer. But after a while the Catholic women used to spit in their tea and call them names. That's how I remember it.

'Even as a kid, I remember looking at the soldiers and thinking, they're not that old. They were only seven or eight years older than me, an average age of about 19. Coverage of the Troubles on the TV intensified gradually. News of beatings and riots became more frequent. It was exciting too, especially before there were any deaths to talk of. At first a lot of young Protestant girls were very taken with the soldiers. It was a real *coup d'état* to nab one of them; even better to get an engagement ring. A girl on our street who was only 14 years old got engaged, and that set a precedent. Every young teenage girl wanted that; you went to bed at night dreaming of marrying a soldier.'

As the Troubles intensified, so too did life at home for Jackie. There are still fuzzy memories of beatings, being picked up and thrown down on the cardinal red tiles that filled the downstairs of Monarch Street. 'Everyone was so stressed out and tempers used to flare. I'm sure many families were the same,' says Jackie. 'I remember specifically being picked up by the back of the neck and knickers and being flung hard on the floor after some empty bottles that were worth a few pence went missing at home. Fred Flintstone and Barney Rubble were arguing on the TV when I passed out. My dad came in later and saw that something was wrong. I was taken to the cinema to make up for it. I couldn't comprehend how I was suddenly looking at Elvis Presley with an ice cream in my hand. My mum cried a lot when I got home and things were fine after that. But I guess, like a lot of homes at the time, it was rocky. My head took a fair few bangs.

'My mum and dad split up before my teens, temporarily at first and then later for good. One day I came home from school and her bags were packed in the scullery. My dad tried to look after us as best he could. A friend of the family, Vivienne Orr, used to call in and make sure we were OK. We also had five or six relations living on Monarch Street, so for a while things ticked over as normal and my dad continued to drive the lorries. At some point his aunt Minnie reported him to the social services because she was worried about us being on our own a lot. Unfortunately her concern seemed to achieve the direct opposite of what was intended.

'Dad was a very good-looking man; women used to swoon over him. To try to help us out, a friend of his called Dora moved in with us for a while so he wouldn't lose us. The only problem was she moved in along with her five kids, so now there were 11 of us in a two-bedroom house. We used to fight for a space to sleep. Dad had to tell her eventually to leave because she was too dirty around the house. After that it became obvious that despite his best efforts he couldn't cope, and myself, my brother and my sisters were sent to a children's home in Portrush.

'I cried a lot because I missed my mum and dad. My dad used to come in to see us but he'd cry a lot as well. The situation was very sad, to be honest. The authorities were aware that he wanted to take care of us and they did try to move us nearer to him. Sometime in 1969 we switched to a home called Child Haven in Millisle, near Bangor. It wasn't a nice place, to put it mildly. The carers were cruel people; they hit us a lot and accused us of having nits and being dirty. We had to call the staff "aunts", aunt this and aunt that—more like anti-children. We used to take ourselves off and do our own thing, playing outdoors for as long as we could. We had our own dormitory. My sisters and I were in one room; my brother was in another. We were there for about a year.

'When my grandfather was dying of cancer late in 1969, my mother came back to Belfast. Dad explained to us that she was taking us to England to live. I started to cry and called him a bastard. He explained that I had to go, that he couldn't give us the life that we needed and was afraid we'd be in homes until we were 18 otherwise. My granddad was buried on a Wednesday morning, and that afternoon a trunk was packed for us and we were off to England. Terry ran away; he didn't want to leave Belfast. He would eventually join us two years later.

'England never felt like home, even if it was a chance of a new start. When my dad stepped off the train two years later, with Terry, he was also accompanied by a woman and her two young boys. I knew then that my dad had found somebody he was serious about. He later married her and went on to have two daughters. Terry moved in with us but he was quite rebellious. I think he was really affected by all the chopping and changing and moving around. He got into trouble a lot and did a few stints in Borstal homes.'

Jackie detested life in England. It was, after all, slap bang in the middle of the 'No Blacks, No dogs, No Irish' era and a lot of Irish families found themselves the targets of abuse and intimidation. The irony for Jackie's family being called 'Irish' is of course all the shoddier when they themselves insisted they were British.

'People were forever calling us "Irish bastards", but my mum was very protective and regularly knocked the crap out of anyone who gave us hassle, even though she's only 4ft 11,' she remembers. 'She'd face Goliath without flinching. The whole family was always like that, fearless. I was a total tomboy, swinging out of trees, running wild on the streets.

'I wasn't clever at school; I was too busy bunking off, going up to the sweet shop at lunchtime and robbing the sweet man. I'd skip piano lessons to go shoplifting; it seemed like a great way to amuse myself. I remember one day bumping into the headmaster when I was out shoplifting in W.H. Smith. He didn't blink an eye when he saw me; I think he had given up all hope for me by that stage.

'I always went back to Belfast during the summer. I'd go back any chance I got. My dad, being a long-distance lorry driver, was living in Worcester. He would pick me up and take me across on the boat or get another lorry driver to take me. Often I would travel over on my own from about the age of 14 or 15, catching the Liverpool boat and staying with relations on the Taughmonagh estate in Belfast.'

When she was 16, Jackie returned to Belfast to live. Ironically, it was on the Taughmonagh estate, where she would one day attract the attention of Johnny Adair, that she met her husband, Billy. 'I stayed with a friend of the family, Vivienne Orr, at that time and helped her with her six young kids. Vivienne's marriage ended, so she upped and left in the middle of the night with the kids and moved into a house in Taughmonagh, taking me with her. A few weeks later, I would take the baby, Cathy, for a walk. One day this attractive looking guy stopped me and asked if the child was mine. When I told him it was a friend's baby, he pretended to steal the child and ran off with her, and I had to leg it to catch up with him. I had a baby daughter of my own a year later in 1977 with him and moved back to Birmingham.

'I always wanted to have kids, to be a mother, perhaps because that was my role from a very young age. Coincidentally, my own husband worked away from home, just like my father had, and we rowed a lot. The marriage didn't work out in the end, but we're great friends now. I had a son in 1980. The same themes have been repeated in my life over and over again, and after my marriage broke down, I had to get out. All my life, all I've ever wanted is to love another person and be loved in a loyal way.

'I planned to stay on in Birmingham when the marriage was over. To this day the kids in my own family have stayed on in Birmingham. Sadly, some of them no longer talk to me because of my involvement with Johnny Adair. They assume I am a killer, that I murdered Catholics and somehow became a top UFF woman. No matter how much I have tried to convince them of the actual truth, I have failed, so I don't bother any more.

'When my marriage was over, my daughter was about to start secondary school and my son was 9 years old. I wanted to return to Belfast, but I was prepared to hang on until the kids got older and had finished school. After we sold the house and split the proceeds, we moved into a new council house and the three of us travelled to Belfast for the Easter break. The kids really loved Belfast and after a week they asked if there was any way we could stay on. We returned to Birmingham, but that summer, 1991, it was decision time. The kids stayed with my cousin Julie whilst I sorted things out. Houses were hard to get in Birmingham at that time, so I swapped the keys with friends in Cumbria. I asked them to give me £2,000 for the keys and another £3,000 for all the new fittings. That gave me extra money to move back to Belfast for good.

'A council house was allocated to me in Belfast within a week because I was born in Northern Ireland and told the authorities we were living from day to day on friends' couches. We moved into 10 Malton Rise. I could not have envisaged spending my entire life in England. There's a Madonna song with the lyric:

This used to be my playground (used to be).
This used to be my childhood dream.
This used to be the place I ran to
whenever I was in need of a friend.
This used to be my playground . . .
This used to be our pride and joy.
This used to be the place we ran to.
That no one in the world could dare destroy.

That song really reminds me of Belfast, of everything it stood for. Throughout my life, any time I was depressed or feeling down, I would get great comfort from coming back to Belfast. Everything was changing for us for the better, or so I believed. Of course, I had no idea that this time around, fate would have it in for me big time, and I was about to take a treacherous nine-year roller-coaster ride with Johnny Adair.'

It might be hard for outsiders to grasp why Belfast, a city in sectarian turmoil, whose streets at night were empty and where killers drove around seeking out their prey, where the air echoed to the sound of bombs and where armed soldiers patrolled, could have such a pull on those who had departed Northern Ireland's shores. Yet unlike the socially atomised housing estates and grim streets of England, Belfast retained a sense of community right up until the early to mid-1990s. Even in the most war-torn strongholds of loyalism and republicanism, there was a social cohesion and a collective wartime spirit as families and communities pulled together to survive. Into this strange, paradoxical world stepped Jackie Robinson, and like many attractive young women living among the hard men of paramilitarism, she soon caught the attention of the local terrorist elite.

'I only went with him that first time for a joke, just to get rid of him. He had been hassling me for weeks, so I eventually agreed to go for a drive with him. Johnny was standing with his head down, hands in his pockets, deep in thought. When he saw me coming in he piped up to his mates, "There she is." We had only gone into the club to have one drink and we were heading off to a hotel nightclub afterwards. He followed me out to the car park of the Taughmonagh Social Club, rapped on my window and asked if he could come along for the ride. "Where are you going? Can I come too?" I hadn't given him a second thought in the intervening weeks.

'It was the first time I had seen him up close and I liked what I saw. He was so cheeky and fun looking with big bright eyes and his baseball cap on backwards. To be honest, I couldn't believe anyone was taking an interest in me. To me, this mischievous man in the baseball cap wanting my attention was just a bit of entertainment, and I desperately needed it at the time. It was childish but flattering at the same time. I drove off and left him standing in the car park, yet again.

'It wasn't until a week later that I said "hop in" when he handed me the keys to his Orion and we drove to a local park, Barnett, at the top of the Malone Road. I was going out with a guy at the time. On this occasion I had had a few drinks and he came down and sat beside me. I was really startled. "Would you go out with me?" he asked. He was like a little puppy. I knew that I liked him so I thought, if I go with him tonight, I'll get rid of him. I asked him if he was married and he said no, but I could see by the look on his face that he was lying. "Have you got a girlfriend?" I asked. "I want the truth." He said, "Yeah." I asked did he live with her and he said he did. When asked if he had any kids, he said yes again. It was getting worse by the second. It didn't stop him following me out to the car park again though, and this time he jumped in and we drove off. After hearing that he had a girlfriend and kids, I really just wanted to be rid of him. I wanted to ridicule him a bit and have a laugh about it. I had no idea how much I was going to fall for him.

'I parked the car—the idea was to give him a kiss and leave it at that. As I turned around he had wound the seat down and was lying back like a lord. Not only that, I got an awful shock when I saw what he had in his hand. "Come on, let me, will ye? I've wanted to fuck you since the first day I met you," he said. I told him where to get off, that I wasn't like that. "Do you think I'm some sort of a slut?" I roared, as I started the car and drove off. I pulled into the car park, threw the keys at him and walked back into the club, leaving him sitting there. It's flattering whenever someone fancies you, but I certainly didn't want this pup getting the wrong idea about me because I had blonde hair and a short skirt. Surely he wasn't that stupid?' Of course, in the long run that only served to make him more determined to have me.'

Another short black dress and Friday night later, Adair made his move with a bottle of Carlsberg Special Brew, and the thorny fairytale in the paramilitary palace was set in motion. During the early stages of the affair, Johnny was going with a few girls at once (including an RUC man's wife) and assumed Jackie knew about them, but she didn't. 'There was one girl from Lisburn, an absolute stunner that I knew about,' explains Jackie. 'I thought she was so beautiful looking. He was also with another woman, Donna, who later became a friend of mine. She had gone out with Johnny for quite a while. He brought her to parties when Gina had planned on being there too. Donna and I used to have a laugh about it when we became friends. She said that at one such party Gina approached her and asked if Johnny didn't have money and fancy cars would she be interested in him. Donna is straight as a die, and simply replied, "Probably not." And that's the base reality —women wanted these men because they were a mix of legendary and loaded.'

Jackie was not widely liked or taken seriously by Adair's caste initially. They were well accustomed to his whoring around and paid little attention to the eye-catching mother of two who seemed nothing more than a harmless fling. If he spent the night at her Taughmonagh home, an early-morning house visit would see several men army march straight into her bedroom uninvited, hauling Johnny by the scruff of the neck without so much as a glance at her. Their attitude changed when she turned down Johnny's offer of money to help out with her living expenses. After four or five months, his cronies began to realise that their relationship was a bit more serious.

'It was months into the relationship when we began to take more risks and started socialising more together as a couple,' she recalls. 'We were fast becoming an item, and I guess his mates twigged that he had dropped other women to be with me. At the same time Gina, who had her spies working overtime, would miraculously turn up at shebeens [illegal drinking dens] where Johnny and myself were drinking, and just stand there and stare. I later learned that her undercover scouts would ring and say to her, "The blonde one is out. Get your coat and go."

'Johnny was an attention seeker and an exhibitionist when it came to women. We were at a shebeen one night and this girl came strolling down the stairs. She's a nice girl actually from the Shankill area. Johnny looked at her, and in an attempt to impress me said to her, "Isn't it right, you were the first one I gave it to over the pool table?" The poor girl went bright red. I went ballistic and shouted, "Don't talk to her like that. Apologise now." And he did. I never let him away with anything. He always tried to be the big boy. He would say or do anything if he thought it would get a laugh.

'We would often be out and if I went to the bar or the toilet, on my return there would constantly be one or two women whispering in his ear. I would watch these women closely. He would look up at me and smile and tell them where to go. I felt that I had some power over him. Maybe because I took control sexually meant he kept coming back for more. I do believe that after a while he did fall in love with me.

'Sex was exhilarating with him. He would get so frenzied he'd pull my hair, which I wasn't used to, but generally I got to like anything that turned him on. I had mirror-robes in my bedroom and he liked to watch us having sex. If he wanted sex on the stairs, living room, bathroom, wherever, it wasn't a problem. Sometimes we were like animals, scratching and biting each other. Yet there was always a tender and affectionate side too. I was never ever afraid he'd hurt me. He was at all times gentle with me. I trusted him with my life. I had been so used to hiding my body, but Johnny saw it all and helped me open up in that way. He got rid of all my inhibitions and taught me what buttons I liked pressed. He must have been with hundreds of women over the years, but he said it was never as good as when he was with me.'

Jackie had a keen interest in murderers when she was young, an irony that doesn't escape her 14 years after the Adair affair was first set in motion. She assiduously read true-crime magazines and journals and wondered what made murderers tick. The killer's compulsive need to sadistically dominate victims fascinated her. Reams of magazine stories from the 1960s and 70s told of how serial killers often had unhealthy obsessions with police or authority figures, wanting to defeat the legal system in the jurisdiction where they operated. Ted Bundy had once masqueraded as a police officer, as had John Gacy, the Hillside Stranglers and others. Killers generally like to dupe the defenceless and vulnerable, rarely murdering for profit but for psychological supremacy. They rarely feel sympathy or remorse and hide behind a carefully constructed smokescreen of normalcy.

As a young teenager, the killers Jackie read about included the likes of Mark Rowntree who terrorised Yorkshire at the same time as the Yorkshire Ripper. He callously killed four people, driven by a so-called 'uncontrollable urge', in 1975, while posing as a policeman to gain entry into victims' houses. He hero-worshipped other killers and when he was eventually caught he claimed his only regret was that he didn't 'manage five', the same as his protagonist the 'Black Panther', Donald Nielson.

Many teenagers are attracted to mind-boggling crime stories, and none more so than the cold, calculating slaughter of innocents at the hands of mad men who seemed normal to the people around them. The classic cliché that what a woman looks for most is to love a bad boy has lingered on long past the age of Shakespeare. The parallel between the likes of Mark Rowntree and paramilitary figureheads in Northern Ireland may seem far fetched, but there are comparisons.

Paramilitary chiefs on both sides were notorious for attracting heaps of female admirers. Michael Stone, Billy White, Billy Stobie, and Dominic McGlinchey, the republican 'Mad Dog', had just as many mattress appointments as assassinations to attend to. Adair also liked to adopt 'disguises' reminiscent of many legendary killers. One of his favoured pastimes was to wear a Celtic football shirt when scouting around Catholic areas, as well as dying his hair so as not to be recognised. Although he usually crossed over the peace-line to stake out Catholic homes that his buddies would later visit, for a while at least it was an effective ruse that served its purpose. He had grown up and, some would argue, had been desensitised amid endless sectarian strife at the height of the Troubles.

As a young teenager he joined a right-wing skinhead group and spent his time sniffing glue, fighting 'Fenian skins', and later upgrading to petty crime around the Oldpark and Shankill areas. He worshipped Michael Stone, the lone loyalist gunman who killed three mourners and injured 50 people at Milltown Cemetery, west Belfast, in 1988. The funerals were for three IRA members shot dead by British special forces in Gibraltar. Adair revelled in the fact that Stone 'brought the war directly to the IRA' and later cited the incident as one of his biggest moments of inspiration. However, Stone would go on to describe Adair as a media-addicted, insecure show-off in his autobiography *None*

Shall Divide Us, where he wrote: 'Adair has never cut the mustard as an operator. He was more interested in the fame game than being a true loyalist. He was more interested in the profile his fame would give him than the loyalist cause.'

'Johnny couldn't even beat Casey's drum, never mind lift a hand to someone himself,' asserts Jackie. 'I have to admit that I got on very well with all of C Company. It's almost hypocritical to say, but I found them great friends, just as republicans found similar operatives on their side of the fence. As people, they were very loyal and dependable, and I had the ability to separate the person from the violence they committed.

'I honestly don't feel I have a right to judge anyone in this life, so I try not to. The fact that I knew them all as individuals with their own histories and lives made it somehow different. I was with one of them who was gentle, kind and loving and I saw no anger or hatred in him at all. They were fun loving and generally got on really well. When you're in there in the thick of it, you don't see that the people you're socialising with are malicious enough to pull a trigger or hack someone to death.

'However, that's not to say I didn't know what was going on. Of course I did; I watched the news like everyone else. My heart used to go out to the families of victims on both sides. I used to anonymously send cards to people expressing my sympathy after murders had taken place. The one incident that will haunt me until the day I die was the time the two British soldiers Derek Wood and David Howes were dragged from their car and beaten to death during the funeral of Kevin Brady at Milltown Cemetery in 1988.

'I will never forget the TV coverage of the car approaching the funeral procession and the group of mourners that blocked it and ransacked the car, attacking the two men. It was horrific seeing that replayed over and over again. It was the first time the brutality of the Troubles was filmed in such a powerful way. Yet the men who did that had support within the republican communities and from the women who shared their lives. That's the thing: there is always backing on both sides no matter how wicked the violence in Northern Ireland. Later on too, when I used to visit Johnny in prison, regardless of what the men were in for, there'd be a queue, mostly women, waiting outside the gates of the Maze Prison to support their loved ones.'

There are now more than a dozen websites to connect prisoners with potential soul mates and some sites like prisonpenpals.com receive over 10,000 hits a day. The site lists African, Australian, Belgian, Canadian, Egyptian and English prisoners. It has also listed its first Irish prisoner serving time at Magilligan Prison, Co. Derry/Londonderry. The homepage is literally bulging with ads from prisoners (including murderers) who advertise that, aside from cooking and lifting weights, 'honesty and loyalty is key in life and I know how to treat a lady'. The site's founder, Adam Lovell, admitted on an American TV show that he receives correspondence every day from inmates asking to have their ads removed because they had found that special someone more quickly than they had anticipated. He also claims that death row prisoners in America are literally 'burdened' with email contacts from women who, at the drop of a hat, would be prepared to have a meaningful relationship with them.

'I didn't get into the relationship originally because of Johnny's status,' explains Jackie. 'That didn't impress me, but once I found myself liking him, having fun, the commitment wasn't there and I felt it was an easy situation to be in. I had someone who wouldn't hurt me. I accepted that Gina was part of the equation; he wanted both of us. But I would have found it deplorable if there had been others as well as Gina and myself. That might not make a lot of sense, but there is a recognisable logic to it for anyone who has had a serious affair. A couple of months into the relationship he asked me if I wanted to see photographs of Gina and the kids. I said no. He could never understand that I didn't want to know what they looked like. I didn't want to enter that far into his family unit or home life. He had three children when I met him, Jonathan, Natalie and Chloe. I wanted what we had to be beyond all that so it could remain special.'

—

The year Jackie met Johnny Adair was one of the bloodiest in a decade. Although in January 1992 a new formula was devised for the resumption of political talks, only nine days in the UFF/UDA shot dead Philip Campbell while he was working inside his fast-food trailer on the M1. A month later five Catholic civilians, including a 15-year-old boy, were killed in a gun attack on Sean Graham's Bookmaker's shop on the Lower Ormeau Road. In April, Philomena Hanna (26), a Catholic civilian, was shot dead in the Springfield Road chemist's where she worked. By the end of April, 13 people had been killed and by year end the number had risen to 22.

In August the then Secretary of State for Northern Ireland Patrick Mayhew announced that the UDA as an organisation was to be banned. In November the organisation announced that it was extending its campaign to include 'the entire republican community'. And by 10 November the political talks in Northern Ireland had collapsed with unionists withdrawing indefinitely. On New Year's Eve, the UDA issued a statement that alleged the organisation was to increase its campaign of violence 'to a ferocity never imagined', but the rowdy partying, drug taking and general social bedlam by its top commanders continued.

—

'I didn't really have any concept of how big Johnny was for much of 1992 as he was only then rising up through the ranks at the time,' reveals Jackie. 'I became acutely aware of his status at a party in Sandy Row one night, five months in, when I asked him if it was true he was a commander. My daughter's friend at the time had told me a few stories. He was clearly amused, turned to his pals and said, "Hey, Jackie wants to know if I'm a commander. What do you think of that?" They fell about the place laughing. He turned back around to me and said, "I suppose you could say I am, Jackie" and that was the end of the discussion. I never asked him anything about it again. Most women involved with these men, republicans included, just went along with it and stood by their men no matter what. It's part of our life in Northern

Ireland. No matter what anyone thinks, I cried a lot when people were being killed, especially the innocent ones who died for nothing.

'Johnny was surrounded by characters desperate to prove themselves. One such guy, Snakey—I used to call him Sneaky instead as he was a right creep—was particularly anxious to prove himself. We were out having a drink with Alec Kerr when Snakey told Johnny that he could do "just as good as the boys" and wanted the chance to prove it. Later that night at a party, again in Sandy Row, Snakey asked Johnny if he could join his team, to set him a task and he'd do it. He kept saying, "Please Johnny, just give me a gun and I'll go off and do whatever you say."

'I told Johnny to be careful, that Snakey seemed way too eager, but the lads were in party mood and wanted to play with his head. Some of them suggested that there were several fruits [gays] living in a nearby street and he should get Snakey to go around there and "stiff" them. In the end they didn't test him out. As it transpired, less than two years later, he would try and set Johnny up by planting a gun down the back of his settee. He had been working for Special Branch all along. I was right about him after all. It was very hard to know who to trust. Snakey died of a heroin overdose in the end.

'It wasn't until a serious attempt was made on Johnny's life that it sank in what a big fish he was. I heard his car pull up in front of my house one day at high speed and he ran in ranting like a mad man. He was excited and agitated all at once, so I knew something had happened. He said, "Fuckin hell, the IRA opened fire on my car!" The guy turned out to be an ex-IRA prisoner who was interned in 1971. His friend had been hit in the arm and Johnny narrowly escaped with his life. I nearly had a heart attack. Of course, I knew that he might be a wanted man, but I guess you put blinkers on when it suits. I put my arms around him and told him that I loved him; it was all I could think of at the time. I wanted to protect him and make sure nothing untoward ever happened.

'A few days later he drove up to the house again, this time wearing a bullet-proof vest and he was laughing loudly. He seemed in a jubilant mood. It used to amaze me how it never bothered him that he was a target. I think he took it for granted that I knew about his antics, but I didn't. I only knew what I saw first hand and what I occasionally heard. I hadn't even given a thought to my own home being a target; that he might be followed there and someone could take us out while we were in bed. I know now that my life also was in danger that entire time, but it somehow didn't seem real. We would laugh as we were leaving the house, checking under our cars before driving off. Johnny and I would say, "Ah sure, at least we'll die together." I didn't fully realise how dangerous it was for my kids and me. If the IRA had wished to take out half the leading loyalists, all they had to do was hit my home any weekend. It would have been one hell of a lottery win for them.

'Less than a year in, I knew how significant he was becoming. Although I never asked for details, I would know by his mood if something had "gone down". He used to wear a ring with UFF engraved on it. Raymond Elder, his good friend, gave it to him; he was later shot by the IRA in 1994 walking along the Ormeau Road. Johnny used to sit there, pensive, saying nothing and twiddling this ring; that's when I knew he was worried about something. Sometimes he looked burdened and would say to me, "Jackie, why do I do these things?" The answer was simple. He was egged on by others just like him. I would also know if something had gone wrong because he would just head up to the bedroom and go asleep for the night. I wondered why Gina didn't send anyone out to look for him. I think he relied on me because I gave him a feeling of love and security and he was comfortable with me, really comfortable.

'Other times he would be clearly wound up and excited, running into the house and switching on the TV to watch the news. If he got the result he wanted, he would let out a big lion roar, his face would light up and he'd jump up and punch the air. He would fix his eyes on me then, waiting for a response. I never gave him one. A lot of women in my position didn't look on their men as being responsible for what made Ulster tick: shootings, bombings, beatings, murders—you just switch off. How else could you realistically cope? Yet it was on those occasions when he got a "result" that he'd be particularly wild in bed. The excitement of a hit would affect him sexually.

'The police often sat outside my house, and with the curtains closed, they knew what was going on. They would give us a cheer when we eventually emerged. We would simply wave back in return. I suppose the security forces call that surveillance, but I call it voyeurism. It began to annoy me after a while, especially if they beeped their horns, so I'd pull up my top and show them my tits. That was how Northern Ireland was policed—dirty old men sitting in cars outside people's houses.'

That brand of voyeurism would rear its hideous head much more aggressively for Jackie before the next year was out. In October 1993, Johnny turned 29 and arrived over to her house with a party of top loyalists, as usual unannounced and late. She had no idea it was his birthday but he was, as always, in prime party form. He made a point of acting the lad and asking his mates should he give Jackie a baby. It was a cruel emotional jibe as Jackie had by this time expressed her yearning to bear his child. The para posse stayed until 4 a.m. and Johnny and Jackie spent the night together making love a record number of times.

The next morning at 8 o'clock, Jackie was relaxing with her two children, two nieces and John Crockard, when a distinctive drone was heard outside. She had planned a trip into Belfast city centre that day to get some early Christmas presents. Jackie's son went to the window and his face turned ashen. 'Mum, there's police everywhere,' he told her. Outside, a Land Rover was jammed up against the hall door, helicopters flew above the roof of the house and the whole estate was cordoned off; police and army, including top detectives and forensics, milled around like ants. The neighbours came out in force to fire bottles and ancillary household objects. 'Can't you just fucking leave them the hell alone yeas bastards!' they roared in a deafening chorus. But sleeping with Johnny Adair would ultimately mean never being left alone, not just hounded by the security forces, but eventually being haunted by a lethal predator who viewed human life as little more than a throwaway toy.

She was about to be hauled off to the infamous Castlereagh Holding Centre, famed for its ferocious and brutal interrogation techniques. An Amnesty report the year before had alleged that three women were raped by guards there, although this was resolutely denied by the RUC. Later in 1994 the European Committee for the Prevention of Torture and Inhumane or Degrading Treatment or Punishment called for immediate improvements at Castlereagh. In July 1995 the UN Human Rights Committee recommended it should be closed 'as a matter of urgency'. Jackie would soon be under no further illusions that her lover was anything but a decidedly dangerous criminal and the British justice system was prepared to go to any lengths to get him off the streets.

02 | CARRY ON PARTYING

I absolutely loved taking drugs, an ecstasy tab followed by a few acid tabs. Before my time with Johnny Adair, I had never taken drugs in my life. It made me feel I was in a different world, full of bright lights and happy feelings. It doesn't hit home that you're off your head surrounded by terrorists—they were just ordinary people having a lot of fun.

What better way to pay homage to a 'good' murder than to down ten ecstasy (E) tabs and party for four days solid, setting people's body parts on fire, frying house pets and slashing car tyres? Partying and politics were fruitful partners, but a truly unforgettable party could only happen when a military manoeuvre was successful, when no one was caught and when the IRA were worked up to an unmitigated frenzy.

Mick lay in a drug-fuelled slumber on a couch full of dog hairs during one of these so-called disreputable celebrations. It was entirely his own fault because the one thing you don't do at a party packed with high-spirited nutters who live every day as their last is fall asleep. Johnny carefully tipped petrol up and down his legs in a zigzag pattern in much the same way a diligent baker decorates a cake with icing. The room fell silent while a C Company assassin handed Johnny a lighter. 'Can you not even wait till bonfire night?' someone joked in the background. Mick woke abruptly in mid-burn, bolting straight for the door screaming, 'I'm burning! I'm fucking burning!' Everyone stood at the window clapping and cheering him on. 'It's only the drugs, honestly. Don't worry mate, you're not really on fire, you're imagining it!' However, the mass effort to convince him it wasn't happening was to no avail as there is little room for debate whether or not your legs are cooking alive.

'Johnny flung a bucket of water over him after a few seconds and all was OK,' recollects Jackie. 'He was good that way, always making amends when and where he could. He gave that bloke £70 to buy himself a new pair of designer jeans. Another time, a friend of mine who lived in Conway Court on the Shankill, decided she needed a break and went out on a bender, ending up at a party near where she lived. Dick Dempsey was there; he was very involved in the whole scene at the time. Johnny used to wind his friends up by pretending he was having an affair with Dick, but it wasn't true, at least not at that time. In fact, Dick would later get a bad beating by his own friends after an argument about drugs money. My friend fell asleep at this party and Dick decided to shave her head, and I mean shave it completely bald.

'After he was finished, she looked like one of those World War II concentration camp people. She woke up the next morning and went totally berserk, screaming blue murder and wanting revenge. I wouldn't mind but she had a lovely head of hair. She borrowed a hat and stormed over to Johnny's house. Johnny calmed her down a bit and told Dick he had to compensate her with £500 to buy a decent wig. So, she took the money, wore a hat for about eight weeks and didn't bother her arse buying a hairpiece. In a few months her hair grew back. But you see, you didn't go to these parties without taking a risk. That was the reason you went in the first place, to see what could possibly happen.'

One element of Johnny Adair that often went unnoticed by the media was his apparent generosity when it came to helping some of his more underprivileged neighbours, particularly prisoners' wives who were finding it tough making ends meet. It is a side that Jackie doesn't forget and maintains that there was a very caring and loving side to the terror boss. Apparently, he habitually ran 'wee errands' for the elderly, bought sweets for the kids on the street and never walked by a homeless person without throwing them a few quid. 'Those poor smelly bastards have nothing and this is not the kind of city to be out on the streets', he would say.

'Johnny had a very big heart although, with all the other stuff he was involved in, that bit gets overlooked,' Jackie says. 'For instance, I remember that first Christmas that I knew him, one of the main players was arrested for some murder or other and Johnny made a point of calling around to his wife with bags of groceries and a big turkey. He also gave her £100 to buy booze, decorations, or anything she needed for the kids. Without his help that woman would not have had much of a Christmas that year.

'Another Christmas he phoned me and said, "Jack, you couldn't do me a wee favour, would ye? Go down to this person and get £250 off him and take it to this woman here and make sure she gets it in time for Christmas. The poor bitch has nothing to be getting on with." He held parties every December for prisoners' kids and their wives, everything paid for in advance— alcohol, food, toys, turkeys, Christmas crackers—and he would make sure one of the boys would dress up as Father Christmas and give the kids a giggle. These parties were generally held in small halls like the Highfield on the Shankill. He personally funded all that, even later on from prison.

'From the first year I was with him, I noticed he started carrying big wads of cash, obviously from different deals that were going on, extortion rackets and what not. We never discussed financial matters and I knew it wasn't my place to ask. I relied on my instincts as well as Johnny's body language and voice to know what was going on. He used to call me Mystic Meg because I always told him what was happening; even if I didn't know the exact details, I still knew what was going on with him. He was convinced I was psychic. It was obvious to me that there was a lot of drug dealing taking place and that this was a new lucrative way of making a lot of money.'

From 1992 onwards, drugs fused firmly with paramilitarism in a way previously unseen, and the parties that seemed to 'just happen' became legendary across Belfast and beyond. The Lower Shankill and Rathcoole estates were riddled with E, acid and other amphetamines at this time. A lot of the drugs were peddled by C Company desperadoes, intent on getting rich quick. Militant loyalism was quickly seen as having vast potential as a lucrative business enterprise more than proficient in funding the 'war'. Republicans preferred to levy a rough and ready drugs tax on profits—local dealers paid an agreed amount to commanders in nationalist estates and in return dealers plied their trade discreetly. The UDA, on the other hand, actively encouraged young people to buy E's direct from its sources, many of whom were drug users themselves. The surreptitious sale of narcotics became so widespread that by early 1991 more long-standing members of the UDA, who abhorred the sale and use of drugs, issued a statement declaring their hostility to the sale of drugs and that it would not be tolerated under any circumstances. Despite this, the money-spinning trade continued unhindered and C Company for one gave its blessing for authorised dealers to carry on selling as normal. The punishment for unauthorised dealers was the iniquitous 'six pack'—a set of two bullets delivered in three rounds through the ankles, knees and wrists.

In later years, the UDA used drugs as an excuse to sanction an unorthodox recruitment scheme for younger members. In exchange for paying off drug debts, terrorist demands were met. Young men would hurl blast bombs and Molotov cocktails at police during riots or engage in some other risky venture to clear their debt. For established dealers however, many of whom were either in C Company or linked to it, after transferring some funds directly back into the UDA, the rest was siphoned back into the high-calibre lifestyles of the chief figureheads. Unlike their republican counterparts, who generally remained conspicuous by blending in with ordinary working-class members of the nationalist community, C Company had become particularly captivated by a high-end lifestyle.

The close-knit bunch of grown-up killers who had gone to school together, played in bands together and shaved their heads together were now peddling class A drugs together, driving fast cars, donning 24 carat jewellery and filling their publicly funded houses with de luxe leather sofas and high-end gadgets. Adair himself owned all the latest state-of-the-art stereo equipment in order to play his beloved UB40 as well as hardcore Chicago House music blaring from his speakers. Like other leading figures in the C Company subculture, Adair also kept a large tank of tropical fish. Mad Dog adored his exotic pets and during interviews with journalists often interrupted the narrative to feed his fish. In the early 1990s one correspondent left in Adair's front room at his Hazelfield Street home was alone with the fish while Mad Dog consorted with C Company cronies in the kitchen. Whilst Adair and company were engaged in a sinister whispering game in the back of the house, the journalist shook with fear as he sprinkled fish food into the tank, on Adair's orders. The poor hack was shaking because he feared overfeeding and killing Adair's tropical friends.

Even outside the two-up/two-down council houses of the Lower Shankill, C Company luminaries loved to show off their newly found, crime-financed wealth. White painted wagon wheels adorned the exterior walls; statues including Buddhist figures in Adair's back garden were on display; electric lights modelled on Belfast Victorian gas lamps were bolted down in the mini gardens at the front of their homes adjacent to extended patios and porches built in mock Greco-Roman style.

The *noveaux-terror-riches* of the Lower Shankill also liked to show off their status on the road. The late Stevie 'Top Gun' McKeag, for instance, was addicted among other things to motorcycles and was often seen speeding around the Shankill Road in the latest Japanese high CC model. When he wasn't riding around on motorbikes McKeag would criss-cross Northern Ireland, often in the company of one of his legion of girlfriends, in an expensive 4x4 jeep or people carrier. On the road nothing was too good for the likes of Top Gun and the top boys of C Company.

And just like their wives and girlfriends, the men of C Company positively dripped with gold jewellery. McKeag, for example, wore a mini gold gun hung from a chunky chain around his neck. The solid gold automatic pistol was a 'present' in recognition of his exploits as one of loyalism's busiest assassins.

All of this was a discernible achievement, as the estates where the main players carried on their 'normal' lives were notoriously impoverished. Few if any of them had ever done an honest day's work in their lives. Eventually the loyalist plunge into drug dealing led to jokes on the street that the letters 'UDA' stood for Unlimited Drugs Available. 'Did anyone ever think in their wildest dreams that true loyalist families would be intimidated and burnt out of their homes in the loyalist heartland of the Shankill Road, whilst drug dealers openly and freely operate only yards away?' an anti-drugs flier proclaimed before Johnny Adair's ultimate downfall in 2003.

There are three focal Protestant areas that became C Company party hotspots as well as being family homes. Probably the most notorious is the Lower Shankill, a warren of houses built in the 1960s alongside some more modern homes that replaced a series of tower blocks known in the area colloquially as the 'Weetabix Box'. The estate is decorated with murals which depict key moments of the hostilities, while the paving stones here are painted red, white and blue and a lot of the houses are still bedecked with UDA flags and other loyalist paraphernalia. Ironically, given that it was Adair's lair for so long, he actually doesn't come from the Lower Shankill. He was born and bred in the nearby Lower Oldpark, a labyrinth of Victorian terraces that run from Crumlin Road Jail to the predominantly Catholic Cliftonville area. Adair grew up literally on a borderline—Manor Street was and is the interface between loyalist Lower Oldpark and republican Lower Cliftonville. In the 1970s and early 80s— his formative years—Manor Street was a no-go area after dark; sectarian murders were commonplace on this thoroughfare and the walls around often echoed to the sound of gunfire.

Adolescent Johnny Adair (born in 1963, six years after Jackie) and his clique of neo-Nazi skinhead friends became known around the Oldpark for their bizarre dress sense and questionable music taste. The young cluster of skins who wore 'Hang Nelson

Mandela' T-shirts and had 'white power' tattoos followed bands like the Specials and the Beat, and also formed their own off the wall musical ensemble, Offensive Weapon. Their gigs were renowned for being dire but great fun to watch as they spat at each other on stage and encouraged members of the audience to beat one another up. Adair, also a member of the NF Skinz in the early 1980s, affectionately alleged that if Hitler's campaign to conquer Europe had met with success, he surely would have 'gassed the Taigs' (Catholics) as well when they disembarked on the island of Ireland.

In 1983, Adair took part in one of many National Front (NF) marches in Belfast, where a glut of the NF's following were marginalised teenagers who needed scant persuasion to vent their anger upon any available malicious cause. Accompanying Adair on the march was Donald Hodgen and Sam McCrory (Skelly), both of whom went on to become C Company henchmen. Adair now lives with Skelly in the small town of Troon, Scotland, following his release from the Maze in 2005.

The pet name for these fascist 80s rallies was 'gluesniffers' march' because so many of the participants carried plastic bags lined with toxic glue and spent most of their time inhaling the noxious fumes in between anti-black and anti-republican mantras. Indeed, the official organ of the republican movement ran a headline with a photograph of one of the skins out of his head on glue: 'Sniffing for Britain!'

While the marches were viewed by most as pitiable, the escalation of fascist thugs in the centre of Belfast would eventually lead to real violence. That same year a homeless Catholic man, Patrick Barkey, was beaten to death on the Lower Shankill by three young men who were members of NF Skinz.

Second in line is Tiger's Bay, a hard-line Protestant community in lower north Belfast, not far from Belfast city centre and the docklands. Once a thriving quarter, half of its Victorian housing stock now lies dormant. Many of the more upwardly mobile working-class Protestants moved into safer zones further up the east Antrim coast to dormitory towns like Carrickfergus and Whitehead. Those left behind in this tough but shambolic redoubt even today live in fear of being engulfed by the much larger and tightly packed republican New Lodge. The UDA in this traditional stronghold portrays itself as the defender of Tiger's Bay.

Lastly, there is Jackie's own estate, Taughmonagh, a post-war housing development on the southern edge of south Belfast. Many of its residents used to live in central Belfast in areas such as the Protestant Sandy Row, Ormeau Road and Donegall Road. The green spaces, trees and playing areas belie the fact that Taughmonagh is a hotbed of loyalist anger and alienation from the wealthier suburbs around it. Close to Taughmonagh is the Upper Malone Road, one of the richest parts of Belfast and increasingly populated by Catholic professionals. Their success and encroachment into what was once unionist middle-class territory has increased the sense of loss and abandonment felt just up the road in Taughmonagh.

Taking the piss and wreaking havoc was taken as seriously as the loyalist crusade, and madcap partying took place in one of three venues: well-known loyalist pubs, shebeens or people's houses in these estates. Shebeens were illegal drinking dens that first appeared as a bizarre consequence of the Troubles in the early 1970s, when a lot of the pubs ordinary working-class people drank in (on both sides) were bombed. They were simply places where the community could drink unthreatened because of their exclusive or semi-veiled nature. As well as being social venues, they also provided ample opportunities for fundraising and/or money laundering for innumerable causes.

Political groups on both sides have long campaigned for particular shebeens to be shut down for what they consider a disregard for authority. For instance, in 2003 the Irish Republican Socialist Party (IRSP) in north Belfast demanded the immediate closure of a shebeen it alleged was being used as a base for launching attacks on Catholics travelling from Ligoniel to other parts of Belfast city. Following a meeting with some of the local residents, the IRSP released the following statement: 'The nationalist working-class communities in north Belfast have been thrown to the wolves on the altar of political expediency rather than the British government tackling those responsible for the current level of loyalist attacks. The shebeen operated by the UDA and situated at the junction of the Ligoniel and Crumlin Roads has been open for a number of months now and attacks especially on cars and taxis leaving Ligoniel have increased tenfold.

'For many in Ligoniel daily trips to work, school, and other everyday trips have become a nightmare with residents injured and their cars damaged. The north Belfast branch of the IRSP are asking who is responsible for curbing the opening of these shebeens which are endemic in loyalist working-class communities? Has a special dispensation been given to the UDA to operate these clubs that are a blight on those communities and provide easy access to drink and drugs for young people who often then attack their Catholic neighbours?

'All those political parties and governments who are party to the farce that is the Good Friday Agreement should wake up and smell the coffee, whilst the British government fail to tackle loyalism that is refusing to change, refusing to live beside their Catholic neighbours without attacking them, and choosing the weakest in our society as its victims. All talk of a peaceful future here is fantasy with no basis in reality. The working-class people of Ligoniel are entitled to the same rights of freedom of travel as everyone else and they cannot be written off as a sacrifice to sectarian bigotry.'

Yet the sombre fact is that republican shebeens were just as infamous and just as menacing. Since the advent of the Troubles, loyalists and republicans had seized control of flats, disused small factories, offices and warehouses and had turned them into illegal drinking clubs. For instance, in the Lower Falls district, the Official IRA's shebeen was called the Cracked Cup, where one of its leading figures in the early 1970s, Dessie Mackin, was shot dead during the first feud it fought with the nascent Provisional IRA. Another republican drinking den in Divis Flats—a complex within sight of the Lower Shankill—was called Dr Hooks, where even in the early hours of the morning local republicans put on entertainment including a folk singer who started his early sessions at 5 a.m. to cater for workers coming off the night shift. In the frontline areas all semblance of traditional law and order was breaking down; new forces were filling the vacuum, and they were already constructing an alternative economy to the official one from which many of those like the working class of the Lower Shankill felt excluded. This included the underground drinking den where heavy alcohol abuse was mixed with the ever present threat of violence. What made the Lower Shankill shebeens different, however, from their earlier predecessors, was that in Adair's lair drugs were as widely available as booze.

'I knew Johnny took drugs, but I didn't fully understand the impact they had on him as I didn't take drugs myself for the first while,' says Jackie. 'I was at a Loyalist Prisoners' Association night in Taughmonagh in our first year with some friends, and Johnny was sitting with some of his pals on the other side of the hall. It was a full house so I couldn't see what was going on, except that I knew he was off his head on E. He sat quietly with his head down, pretty much out of it. Gina walked in unexpectedly and sat with him. She didn't take drugs at the time.

'A guy known locally as Coke—another UDA commander—followed Johnny into the toilets and within minutes all hell broke loose. The entire place was in uproar. I saw Johnny whizzing by and his mates running outside. Coke, for a laugh, had put a gun to his head in the toilets and Johnny being so stoned and out of it, took it very seriously as a threat. I ran up to see what was going on and if Johnny was OK. I was very frightened. Men from the estate were running in behind the bar and hiding under tables. Johnny was pacing up and down the corridor, really agitated, and his mates were screaming, "Just fucking shoot him. Shoot him!"

'Coke was well known in his area for terrorising young kids under his control and he used to beat up his wife regularly as well. He wasn't well liked. Guns began to arrive on the scene by the dozen, it seemed. I called a friend over and told him to get Johnny out of the way, as by this time I knew he could be very easily influenced and was capable of doing something crazy. Gina looked completely panicked. No one knew what to do. Johnny left and at least on this occasion a bloodbath was avoided, but Coke did get reprimanded the next day and he never tried it again. A couple of the fellas gave him a good kicking. If you put one step wrong, there would always be a bad beating to contend with.

'The only time things would really go a bit too wild was when drugs were involved. Some of these 'hard men' took up to ten E's a night. At another LPA do around that time, my sister and her husband were visiting from England and we met up at the Taughmonagh Social Club. Johnny met us inside and afterwards we went to the Shankill shebeen. There must have been at least a hundred people there. There was a lot of bantering and slagging going on. A fella known as Mad Dog Jackie, who was like a protector to Johnny, was also there. Raymond Elder was trying his best to tease Mad Dog Jackie by shouting for their rivals, "Up the UVF!" Mad Dog Jackie told Elder if he didn't shut up he'd get shot. I saw Johnny whispering in another man's ear and Mad Dog Jackie was taken out of the way up the stairs. Minutes later he flew back down into the main room and opened fire into the ceiling. My sister and brother-in-law were in a complete panic, and the place was in uproar. That was the type of thing that went on; they were all out of it.

'The shebeens for some reason were more fun. I daresay the fact that they were illegitimate drinking holes added to the sense of excitement. In a way the estates were brought together in the one place, where everyone was connected in their politics and where they all socialised,' says Jackie. 'There were dozens of shebeens throughout Belfast, and there still are. Gown Street shebeen was a favourite haunt; another preferred joint was Wolfland Close shebeen; and there was yet another on the Shore Road. They were scattered all over the place, in garages, community halls, empty houses—any vacant space that could be turned into a drinking den. All you needed was a couple of beer pumps and a bit of spare heat. The routine was usually to meet in one of the main established pubs for a few beers, then move on to a shebeen or two or three, then back to someone's house for a bit of a wacky party.

'At one stage, prisoners' wives were banned from some shebeens as the stress of their husbands or partners being in jail meant the women were going wild in these places most nights, shagging around. These women would only visit the prison in the afternoon. It was called the "embarrassing time", because their mornings had been spent with a lover. But because everyone was drinking and off their heads, if anyone went off with a woman whose man was locked up, they would get a beating. Because this was happening so often, the women were banned.'

'Taughmonagh Club was good on a Sunday night as there was a disco and it was always packed. Billy Carroll was the DJ there and he was fantastic. The Shankill ones came to that a lot, but people came from all over Belfast too. There was hardly ever any hassle in that place, despite what some would call a dodgy clientele. We drank in Dan's Bar in Roden Street. Johnny rang me from there one time like a kid all excited because he had dyed his hair white. "Jack, come and meet me. You should see the hair. It's pure white!" He was quite vain, always worried about how he looked. Well, when I walked in and saw the state of him. It's no wonder he likes Marilyn Monroe because he looked like a blubber version of her. "Do you not like it?" he asked, all concerned. After a while he jumped up and starting shouting, "Ah for fuck's sake!" A sachet of the hair dye that was in his pocket had leaked down to his skin. He stood up and pulled down his boxer shorts, and hadn't his arse hairs turned blue from the stuff. "Blue is a good royal colour, Johnny, don't worry about it," I said. He just laughed and got some more drinks in. "Lads I've got a blue hole!" he roared out of him. He had a great sense of humour. That's the only thing I miss.

The first time Jackie got really stoned was when a can of diet coke she left down on a window-sill at a party was spiked with four acid tabs by some of Johnny's friends who were eager to see how drugs would affect her. Jackie was a bit of an anomaly on the social scene. Up until then she rarely drank, didn't take drugs, but still managed in the eyes of many to be suitably nuts and fit in fine with the most boisterous of them. It was quite a baptism of fire as acid is a powerful hallucinogenic drug that alters a person's perception of the outside world. During the course of an acid trip, colours become deeply intense, everyday objects take on bizarre and astonishing new forms, while most of the five senses are distorted and bent out of shape. It is a gradual high, taking from 20 minutes to two hours to take effect, with trips typically lasting around 8 to 12 hours. There's no real way of knowing how strong a tab is or how exactly it will impinge on a person's mind.

'Imagine, the first time you take drugs, you accidentally take four of the fucking things!' muses Jackie. 'I had no idea what was happening to me. We were at a party on the Shankill and before I drank all the diet coke the usual bantering was going on. They ripped off this guy's clothes and flung him out on the street naked and wouldn't let him back in—that kind of thing. He was lucky though, because what they usually did was force the naked person into a car, drive off with him and dump him on a motorway, where he'd have no choice but to keep walking until someone gave him a lift home. Now, who was going to stop for a buck-naked man late on a Saturday night in Belfast at the peak of the Troubles? So all this stuff was going on and I could feel my mind going a bit odd. Colours were changing and people's faces were becoming distorted. I looked over at one woman and saw a skeleton sitting there laughing. I didn't know if it was some kind of bizarre premonition or if I had lost my marbles. I made my excuses and went home. As soon as I arrived, the phone rang and it was Johnny and his mates. "You're off your fucking head on drugs. We spiked ye!" one of them said, so I called him a bastard, although I was laughing, and jumped into bed to sleep it off.'

The world was a much better place for Jackie on drugs, much cleaner, brighter, safer and more pleasurable. It was a way to opt out of life for a few hours at a time and play a part in an outlandish stage drama where the actors didn't care if there was an engrossed audience or not. Drugs became a way to blend in, to be accepted, to feel normal. 'One night, a friend called over and asked me to drive him down to Charlie Hegarty's in Bangor. It was a really big venue and had a great disco. I said no problem and took a few friends along for the ride. I took just one E, but for some reason it seemed to be loaded with acid; they were getting stronger all the time. I began to hallucinate really badly and had to be driven back to Belfast.

'We headed to the Midland Close shebeen and this wee old man came up to me—he was 60 years old—and he says, "Oh love, they've given me a microdot and I'm having a heart attack. Can you help me?" I asked him if he had ever been on drugs before and he said this was his first time, so I told him not to panic, it was just his heart rate increasing and that he'd be fine. Someone told me afterwards that he died a few weeks later. In the meantime, my mind was coming undone and I thought we were all wee mice looking for a tree we could set up home in. The boys were making lots of farmyard noises so I really thought we were on a farmstead. They kept saying, "What's that, what's that? Oh it's just a bunch of geese and some miniature sheep looking for some lady's legs to keep warm." I believed every word of it. A woman at the side of the dance floor kept smiling over at me; she wore bright red lipstick and looked quite threatening. I said, "That fucking lady there keeps staring at me. I'll knock her block off", but it was actually my sister Kim.

'It got a bit more sinister as the hours went by and I wouldn't let anyone go to the toilet, being convinced some of the head men were going to throw us in a wheelie bin and shoot us. By that time the paramilitary angle had reared its head and I suppose everything I used to feel subconsciously with Johnny was coming to the surface. I accompanied every person that went to the toilet, male or female, and stood there while they relieved themselves, certain I was saving their life. Of course this only convinced some of the more serious jokers that I was a great target.

'When I was a kid, there was a programme on the TV called *Teatime with Tommy*. For some reason on this particular night I thought we were all on the programme when I saw everyone dancing and imagined they had big long jumpers on and old men's caps, all happy and smiling. Yet I couldn't get it out of my head that we were all going to be shot. Two of the men took me home when they realised just how far gone I was, but even back at the house they continued to wind me up. Brian kept moving the phone nearer to me and telling me that Special Branch (SB) were going to phone me shortly and I'd need to keep a straight head. "If that phone rings and it's the SB," they told me, "it's a clear indication Jackie that you might have to die." I was absolutely petrified, but you see, by the next morning you'd be pissing yourself laughing remembering what a dickhead you had been the night before. One of their favourite tricks was to wait until someone went to the toilet, then they'd run about at great speed changing all the furniture around in the room and turning pictures upside down, just to confuse the victim. Needless to say it was great fun to watch as long as you weren't the butt of the joke.'

The comical adaptation of changing rooms also applied to 'demolishing' rooms just as easily, as Jackie once found out on another occasion when she and a bunch of the lads had partied for three days solid without any sleep. As the happy bunch of midnight revellers hadn't eaten a morsel for days, she offered to make them some breakfast back at her place. She had just had her house done up, spending thousands kitting out the sitting room and knocking down a wall between the kitchen and the main room. She had spared no expense with the furnishings; the settee alone cost £500 and the fluffy new carpet was the equivalent of three months' wages. Just as they were sitting down to their meal, the coal man arrived and some of the men ran out and began robbing sacks of coal off the back of the van. Not surprisingly, even though the coal man saw what was going on, he wasn't about to complain when he saw who they were.

After stocking up Jackie's shed with a whole winter's supply of free fuel, one of the men threw a load of coal on the fire, lit it and just when it had reached a hearty scarlet glow, he threw a couple of Jackie's asthma inhalers on to the flames, quickly replacing the fireguard. When Jackie came in from the kitchen, she was greeted with a horrendous blast, and the new carpet and settee burst into flames. The unprompted breakfast show turned out to be a powerful little homespun bomb.

'The entire room was totally ruined,' she reminisces, 'but I just started laughing my head off. Within ten seconds the room had been completely destroyed.' Johnny footed the bill for a second round of house renovations. 'Well I couldn't let the fuckers get away with it now, could I?' she explains. 'I had worked really hard to save up that money; I had two cleaning jobs at the time and helped out at an Alzheimer's care centre. I was bringing up two kids on my own and deliberately never took money off Johnny, no matter how much he offered me.'

Another favourite pastime at parties was to convince one of Johnny's more devoted followers that news had come through from a reliable source that he or she was a tout, an informant, a leak, a grass, a spy. This was at all times a serious allegation, not really something to joke about. Touts were Johnny's single biggest revulsion. In the early 1990s a number of 'strange occurrences' pointed towards the existence of touts within the UDA. At a time when gun running was an almost hermetically sealed activity, a batch of SA-80 rifles was discovered by the police in Belfast in what Adair was convinced was a tip-off. Other surveillance operations had to be called off when consignments of police seemed to miraculously appear as Johnny and his boys were scouting around nationalist areas doing their pre-murder research.

Adair was always particularly perplexed about his thwarted attempts to shoot dead the man who commanded the IRA in Belfast between 1990 and 1994. The west Belfast-based republican had been a prime target for Adair partly because he was responsible for a three-year bombing campaign aimed at blowing the commercial heart out of the city. This man was also a principal target for the RUC Special Branch who arrested him on numerous occasions. While in Castlereagh Holding Centre, however, the IRA commanding officer maintained a Trappist-like silence. His one and only response to his RUC interrogators, on being asked what he did for a living, was 'I make car parks'—an allusion, no doubt, to his and his bombing team's ability to lay waste tracts of Belfast. There was one exceptional incident, however, when the IRA O/C's wall of silence cracked. Under pressure from Adair's unit, having been the target of several aborted assassination bids and having attended the funerals of republican comrades that C Company had gunned down, the IRA's Belfast leader reacted violently when the RUC taunted him about Mad Dog. In response to the police officer's predictions that Adair would get him, the Provo boss (who is now a member of the seven-man IRA Army Council) lost his rag and screamed: 'I'll get that wee bastard. I'll get him.'

Neither did Adair get him. In 1993, for instance, Adair led a unit comprised of his old chum Skelly and another C Company veteran. They had taken over a house in the republican Lower Andersonstown area of west Belfast on the pretext that they were the local IRA about to launch a gun attack on a British Army patrol. Adair and his unit had to wear long-sleeved shirts to cover up their loyalist tattoos to maintain the masquerade. The unfortunate family involved in the house takeover believed they had let in a local IRA unit. In fact Adair and his group were planning to assassinate the IRA O/C, who, thanks to high-grade intelligence from a rogue British soldier in the Royal Marines, used a safe house in the street. At the expected time of the IRA man's arrival, the C Company squad cocked their rifles preparing to run into the street and gun down their target. The IRA boss did indeed appear, but within seconds the street was flooded with British troops who stopped and searched the leading Provo. Adair later confessed that someone had touted or informed on the audacious operation right in the heart of Gerry Adams's constituency. The IRA man's British enemies had saved his life. It was a bitter irony too for Adair, because it had been a British soldier who had led them to the IRA officer's safe house, and yet it was the arrival of other British soldiers that had spared the republican's life. Informing and collusion were often double-edged swords that sometimes brought results and at other times halted or compromised high-profile hits.

Such was his contempt for touts that Johnny used to remark that no amount of torture was adequate and death was too weak a solution for a shameless snitch. 'Johnny used to say, "Once a tout, always a tout', and would never forgive a person for grassing to the peelers [police]," says Jackie. 'He got so paranoid about touts that I think deep down he didn't trust anyone. There were often times I thought he protested about touts just a little too much, and that maybe he was trying to hide something himself. Yet at parties the whole tout thing was a great excuse to get completely out of hand. What they would do was pretend they were taking a call and call Johnny over to a corner, whispering frantically and staring over at someone at the party. And then

Johnny would say, "I just have to step out for a moment", and he'd give the nod to another guy in the room to go over and tell the chosen victim that they had received information that he was a tout. They would then come back in and accuse the bloke of being "wired", take him out to the back garden, tell him they were going to shoot him if any surveillance equipment was found on him and strip him. You would never know if they were joking or not because they'd keep it up for ages. "We know you're working for MI5, so you may as well spill the beans," he'd scream, and the innocent victim, out of his head on drugs, would start pleading, "No, it's not true. It's a bunch of lies. Please Johnny, please." Eventually they'd break their arses laughing. "We had ye there, mate. You thought you were going to meet your maker."

'There was a party in Coke's house early in 1993. The postman and his wife were there. They waited until the postman was really off his head before winding him up, saying the UFF were going to kill his wife. She had gone home a bit earlier as she felt sick. This poor guy took them seriously; there was no convincing him otherwise. They told him that his wife had been taken to another city "to be dealt with". When he went to the toilet and came back, they had done their usual trick of changing the furniture around and he looked even more confused. "Ah, there's something wrong here," he kept saying. "Why, what's wrong mate?" Coke asked him, but he just headed off. It turned out that he went all the way to Dublin to try to find his wife, certain her life was in danger. He didn't come back for three days. That's how much the drugs affected him. Just after he left, one of the other men who hadn't been home to his wife in three days ran into the sitting room and said, "She's looking for me lads, she's looking for me." She was at the door with a hatchet and was going to hack the door down if they didn't let her in. They thought this was hilarious. They hid in the loft. They wouldn't let her in and the bloke was too scared to go home until he was sure she had got rid of the hatchet. The women were quite feisty too; I suppose living with these men they had to be.'

Incredibly, no one was ever seriously maimed or killed at these parties. This was during a rare time when the UFF overtly mixed with the UVF (Ulster Volunteer Force) and everyone got on really well and abandoned their usual enmity, according to Jackie.

Her account of on-the-ground UVF/UFF collaboration and camaraderie was not shared with the upper stratum of the former organisation. Most of the UVF leadership further up the Shankill Road were men from an older generation, many of whom worked for a living, and some of whom had been trade unionists, and due to their socially conservative outlook despised and feared the burgeoning drug culture further down the road in Adair's heartland. Rightly or wrongly, the UVF regarded themselves as the true inheritors of the original Ulster Volunteer Force set up by Sir Edward Lord Carson to resist Home Rule in the early twentieth century. They perceived themselves as a 'People's Army' run on the same organisational lines as the British Army with brigades, an officer class and even an internal military court system. In reality the UVF, just like the UFF, during the Troubles committed heinous sectarian atrocities, the most appalling of which were the Shankill Butchers killings. This gang, semi-autonomous from the UVF high command, prosecuted a reign of terror against the Catholic communities of north and west Belfast from the mid to late 1970s. Their *modus operandi* was to kidnap lone Catholics walking through central and north Belfast at night, take them to loyalist shebeens and self-styled safe houses, torture their victims and then shoot or beat them to death.

None the less there was at leadership and middle ranking level a qualitative difference generally between the UVF and the new UFF kids on the block—so much so in fact that Johnny Adair and his chums mocked the alleged inactivity of the UVF in the loyalist murder upsurge of the early 1990s. Adair and his friends labelled the UVF 'the Peace People' because the older loyalist movement had been known to send overtures to republicans and the Irish government over a possible ceasefire. Any socialising between the UFF and UVF foot soldiers was normally frowned upon by the latter's leadership, comprised in the main of men in their late 30s, 40s and 50s, who believed that Adair and C Company were loose cannons out of control.

At a party in a commander's house in Sandy Row, a close

friend, who was involved in another organisation, sauntered into
the couple's kitchen with their goldfish in his mouth, pretending
that he was starving and was going to scoff it. The commander's
wife, who adored the goldfish, went bonkers, screaming and
shouting for him to put it back. Some of the lads were egging him
on, but not wanting to rile the big man, conceded and put the
dishy fishy back in the safety of his bowl. Not long after, the E's
came out and within an hour, when the big man's wife came back
into the kitchen, the goldfish was frying (live) on the pan to a
round of raucous laughter. 'His wife ran about in tears
threatening people,' says Jackie. 'She was totally upset about this
goldfish; she really loved it. But that's the kind of thing they
would get up to. They force-fed a budgie some acid another time
and let it fly about the room off his wee head.'

The party at the big man's house also managed to humiliate
one of the better known hanger-on women who had been lusting
after a certain married man for some time, except on this night
his wife was there to witness her advances. After a glut of drugs
had been consumed, the wife tiptoed behind the woman as she
sat on the couch smiling coyly at her husband, sprayed half a can
of hairspray over her head and lit a match. 'All of a sudden, she
realises her hair is on fire and she's patting it like crazy, screaming
for help,' says Jackie. 'We were on that many drugs we thought it
was brilliant, and just kept laughing all the more. The woman
started to cry, and this man's wife told her to piss off if she
couldn't take a joke, and booted her out the door. We were
looking out the window laughing as she walked down the
pathway, her hair smouldering away.'

Jackie was ostracised by some of the men, however, who felt
that she was leading their wives astray. Even if the men were free
to party like demented animals, sleep around, sell drugs and
commit the odd murder, the women were expected to be slightly
more composed and predictable. A lot of the men went with
Catholic girls because they lived in far-flung estates and their
wives were less likely to find out about them. 'Paramilitary
groupies', as Adair called them, were both a source of
entertainment and a much-needed escape or distraction from the

constant strain of the conflict. According to Jackie, there was no shortage of Catholic girls who were willing to travel the gauntlet from nationalist estates like Andersonstown and Ardoyne to drink in loyalist pubs and shebeens. This may surprise anyone who is not overly familiar with life, love and politics in Northern Ireland, given the 'us and them' nature of the conflict. This was after all the era of ACWD (any Catholic will do) when it came to murder, yet some of those involved were going out with Catholic women or married to them. Raymie Elder's wife was a Catholic and Cathy Spruce, Adair's ex-girlfriend-turned-tout, was Catholic. The incongruity was down to the fact that the war was against republicans, not Catholics, although Adair often strategically blurred those lines, as Jackie would later find out when they went on their nocturnal outings to the Falls Road and other Catholic areas. Yet even the late night reconnaissance missions weren't totally devoid of a bit of fun. Johnny and Jackie would often jump out of a car in the middle of the Falls Road and take a quick wee in full view of enemy lines. The message, even if innocuous, was simple, 'We'll piss on your patch as well as kill you.'

'They knew what they were dealing with when it came to Catholic or Protestant, friend or foe, but some of the men didn't like the fact that I was totally unknown, that I seemed to blow in from nowhere with my short skirts and blonde hair, and I was fearless. I didn't take crap from any of them, not for a second, and they weren't used to that,' says Jackie. 'I had been through this personal transformation and I had real confidence probably for the first time in my life, and no shithead was going to get rid of it. I could see that some of their wives had been ground down over the years and I'd try to encourage one or two of them to dress different, to start liking themselves again, to get out there and have a bit of fun. The men didn't like that one bit.

'The commander on Taughmonagh in particular didn't like me. He commented to a friend of mine that he thought I was a "right slut" because of how I dressed. It was a bit of a no-win situation really, because when I was first on the estate a lot of male attention was coming my way and some men saw this as shameful and some of the women didn't like it. I really didn't think I was anything much, but the boys thought otherwise. For a while it seemed that everyone was trying to make moves on me. This particular commander's wife made it clear that the estate was her territory and that I was to keep my hands off the boys. She was constantly bitchy towards me, but I used to say to her, "Go fuck yourself, lady." I truly didn't care. It was as if I'd been put down in Birmingham for so long that when I got back to Belfast I was determined to live my life as I wanted, but these women in general didn't like that. It was all about status. The commander's wife would have had other women following her about, licking her arse so to speak, and they all wanted to sit with her in the pub, to be associated with her supposed power. I couldn't care less, and maybe at times this was seen as disrespectful.

'At the same time I fitted into this crazy new life like a hand in a glove. It was just fun to me. I knew there was serious shit going on. I've had people say to me since: "It must have been a power thing with you", but it wasn't. I just felt I was living for the first time in decades. It wasn't all shiny and happy though. When I started going out with Johnny some of my friends dropped me; they got scared about him being around. I couldn't understand that. A couple of the women were having affairs and their husbands knew, but they were blaming me, saying their wives had never gone out to parties until they met me.'

Despite this, after the first year Johnny's mates became quite endeared to Jackie and would even come to her workplace and drag her away for some fun. 'I worked in the Tudor Lodge at one stage and I really loved it. I did all the shifts at the weekends. I was a bar woman and I also worked in the restaurant. On Friday nights there was a disco and a lot of the heads would come in. I'd take only £1 off them for a tray of drinks, but the management never complained. One night Winkie Dodds, Johnny's closest friend for a long time, came in and said, "You're coming to a party, you need a good night out, a night off from all this work." He said to Raymond, the manager, "Look, mate, she's leaving now to go to a party. She's not cleaning up, you can clean up yourself." Everyone stared at Raymond to see his reaction. He knew who

Winkie Dodds was. His response was no surprise: "No problem, mate. No problem at all." On the way there Winkie turned to me and said, "You know what I like about you, Jackie. You know what we are and who we are, but you treat us like people, like human beings." A lot of people were too scared of these people to see any other side to them apart from the brutal aspect. Yet they were also leading normal lives, worrying about their kids at school, who was getting a bad time on *Coronation Street*, where they were going on holidays.'

Being associated with Johnny Adair's close sect meant not only that all your drinks and drugs were paid for at the bar, but also local take-aways, taxi fares and other local services and amenities. 'I often went out with just £2 in my pocket and came home with over £100,' says Jackie. But other unusual benefits seeped through even down to the level of local government and housing departments. 'Anytime I wanted to move, usually to be nearer to Johnny, I'd get a new house within a week or so of requesting one. The estates were predominantly full of people whose families were involved in the struggle in some way or other, so the housing people didn't argue about wanting to move between addresses,' says Jackie.

It wasn't unusual at the time either for policemen and members of the security forces to attempt to ask out some of the women who were involved with some of the main figureheads. Jackie maintains that she was often asked out by these men in an obvious attempt to find out crucial information about their activities.

'The shebeens were regularly raided and on one occasion a policeman took a bit of a shine to me, or so he wanted me to believe,' she explains. 'I was dancing away when they came flying through the doors at the front and back of this shebeen, a once empty house. "Nobody move!" they roared. I knew we were going to be searched and I had drugs on me, so I said to my friend, "Do you want some of these or what?" and handed her two E's; I swallowed two as well. They had male and female officers ready to start the searches, but I started joking along with them saying, "Would yeas not just try and relax a bit and join in the fun?" One of the policemen started smiling away at me; he was actually quite horny looking, if I'm being honest. I was searched to no avail and my details taken.

'A week later I was in the Elbow Room on the Dublin Road and that same friend and I were heading over to the Alex Bar on the Shore Road. I heard a Land Rover buzzing down the road after us. He had watched us getting into the car and had driven around the block to catch up with us at a junction near by. When he stopped us I realised it was the same one from the shebeen. He said, "So where's that tattoo of yours, Jackie, that I heard about?"—I have a panda tattoo on my bum. The following week he stopped me again, except this time he asked for my phone number, suggesting we go for a drink. He was young, in his early 30s and very attractive. Of course he only did it to see if I was gullible enough to divulge information, but it wouldn't have been worth my life to start double dating with a cop, so I told him where to go. I got asked out by members of the security forces at least a dozen times during those years. All the women close to these men did.'

The first time Adair told Jackie he loved her, albeit in his usual droll and witty way, turned out to be the same day the security forces began their bulky intelligence file on her. It was a Saturday evening in July 1992 at the Kimberley Bar during another LPA get-together. Johnny was standing at the bar supping special brew with all the usual suspects from south Belfast: Raymie Elder, Joe Bratty, Coke and others, and as soon as she entered the bar, his eyes lit up 'like a wee child's' and he started bragging to his mates, 'See her fellas. I fuckin' love her, I do! Just look at her, look at those legs!' Jackie wasn't sure if he was teasing or not, but it still made her feel good. It had been a long while since she felt so enamoured by a man.

'We were feeling frisky so we decided to leave a bit early, but just as I was about to drive off, the car was surrounded by peelers. I was driving Johnny's white Orion. An RUC man tapped on the window and told us to get out. "Open the boot!" he instructed. Johnny said to him, "I don't know why you want to check the car. There's nothing in it." Johnny stood there with his hands in his pockets and his head hanging down low, like he always did when he was thinking. Some of the boys got wind of what was happening and came out of the bar, determined to give them grief. "Let them alone. What are you doing?" they shouted. "Piss off and go hassle some IRA pricks instead." The cops, knowing the shit was going to fly, let us drive off, but they followed in a police car. When I indicated left, they indicated likewise behind me. I carried on and indicated left again, but actually turned right and flew down the Ormeau Road. But there was a gang of them down at the embankment at the Ormeau junction and they surrounded us. Johnny was wearing the UFF ring that Raymie Elder gave him. He kept twisting the ring in silence. When we got out of the car, Johnny started riling them a bit, blowing about who he had [supposedly] shot and who he was going to shoot. I said to him, "Johnny shut it", but they were egging him on. They took all my details before we left. Back in the car he was totally quiet. There was sadness in his eyes, as if he was asking himself, is this really worth it? We went for one drink only and he came back to my house. I had a stereo in the bedroom. He loved to listen to reggae as he was going asleep. "I just want to go to sleep, Jack," he said. He wasn't in the mood for sex, I could tell. I told him I was going to drive to the local garage to get some electricity credit. I had no sooner left my estate when they stopped me again. They had set up a road-block only 50 yards up the road, letting all the other cars pass except Johnny's Orion. "Do you know whose car you're driving?" they asked, and I told them it was a fucking stupid question, as if I didn't know whose car it was, would I be sitting in it? Are you involved with the owner of this car? What business do you have in this car?—all kinds of dumb questions. That was the beginning of their surveillance file on me, and it would be constant harassment from that time on.

It's likely that the police at the time thought Jackie was more involved than she actually was. For every attempted 'operation', help was needed and women usually provided it—safe houses to return to after a hit; washing clothes to get rid of forensic evidence; storing guns, providing alibis etc. Unknown to Adair at the time, Jackie had already acquainted herself with the higher echelons of the UDA by helping to carry out an infamous gun-running operation within a year and a half of returning to Belfast. The brigadier of south Belfast had approached her and asked if she would take part in the operation as she was relatively unheard of.

'I met him and a friend at a spot not many people went to at the time,' she recalls. 'He asked me would I go across to England and take this other person with me. The plan was to have guns brought to Birmingham and that this other person would pick them up and make his way back to Belfast. I would be a type of go-between. I was told that I would be given money to buy a car, and the guns which would come from London were to be placed behind the front bumper. When asked about a safe place, I gave him the name of a park I knew up at Perry Barr, a huge place where the grounds go on for miles. That was our pick-up point.

'At 3 p.m. that day, after we had pulled up at the pick-up point, I had a feeling something was wrong. I told the guys I didn't think it was a good idea to pick up; we had already waited half an hour and there was no sign of our London contact. One of the men I was with put in a call to Belfast on his mobile. In the car mirror I could see two men walking with a holdall. They walked past the car and sat down a few yards away, making no attempt to approach us. They kept turning the holdall at different angles, which didn't make much sense, so I decided to drive off.

'I made my way home on the Sunday morning via Stranraer. The second pick-up was to be 12 noon on Monday at a car park in the grounds of a pub in Perry Barr. On the way up the motorway the car starting playing up; I managed to pull in at a motorway station. I rang my dad and he picked me up and took me to the boat. I later learned that my brother Terry had turned the car over to the anti-terrorist squad as he was suspicious about my trip to Birmingham with "these people".

'On the Monday, the fella I had been with made his way to meet the two London contacts and pick up the guns, but unknown to them both the London man was being tracked by an anti-terrorist team. The guns were placed in the car as planned, but within minutes they were surrounded by police who jumped on the bonnet of the car and on the roof pointing Kalashnikovs at the three men. One of the men from London had been working with Special Branch. My friend from Belfast got six years, Eric Portinari got eight years and the tout got four. I'm not proud of my part in it, but shit happens. I've escaped prison a good few times now.'

Portinari was a personal friend of John White, the UDA multiple killer who after his release from jail on licence in 1991 became a father-figure to Adair. Born a Catholic and of Italian extraction, Portinari drifted into the British far right as a wayward teenager and struck up a friendship with Ulster loyalists whom many in the National Front and other fascist micro-groups came to identify with. What perhaps Belfast did not know was that Portinari by the early 1990s had also struck up a friendship with an agent for the South African Apartheid regime, Leon Flores, who was engaged in a dirty tricks operation against anti-White Rule intellectuals from South Africa based in Britain. Flores via Portinari sent bogus intelligence to the UDA, hinting that Queen's University Belfast lecturer and anti-apartheid writer Dr Adrian Guelke was a secret link between the IRA and the African National Congress. Armed with false information, the UDA went and almost killed Dr Guelke in 1991. Flores was later deported from the UK due to his activities, while Portinari and his London UDA brigade were betrayed by informants after the gun smuggling operation was compromised a year later. Jackie had a very lucky escape!

It is only in recent years with Jackie off the scene that she has come to realise just how scared her neighbours were, but no one dared complain. The constant trepidation they felt wasn't just about the parties getting out of hand or something going wrong, but that if the IRA came to get them they could mistakenly bomb or shoot at the wrong house. It was hardly an unrealistic fear. There were at least ten attempts on Johnny Adair's life during the years she was involved with him. They included two separate attacks on his home in Hazelfield Street, one by the Provisional IRA, the other by the Irish National Liberation Army (INLA). Adair even caught the attention of a lethal British Army undercover unit operating in secret throughout Belfast in the late

1980s and early 90s. Mad Dog and one of his oldest friends, Big Donald Hodgson, narrowly escaped death in 1993 after Adair challenged a scraggy-looking, tramp-like figure who kept appearing outside the door of his home. When Adair eventually sidled up to this mysterious character, the man drew a gun and fired at the C Company boss and Hodgson. Adair dived out of the way while a bullet appeared to hit Big Donald in the stomach. In fact the bullet bounced off a belt buckle which probably saved his life. It was at moments like this when Jackie and those close to Adair wondered if Mad Dog was more like Mad Cat with the yet-to-be-paid nine lives.

By 1992 and into 1993, C Company had become famous for their ruthless killing of 'soft targets' and increasingly the security forces were being directed to 'do something', anything to get these men off the streets. C Company used the characteristic shock tactic of indiscriminate killing to bring the war to the attention of ordinary people and their IRA opponents. In December 1992 the UFF carried out seven incendiary bomb attacks on shops in Dublin and other Irish towns near the border, claiming that the war had extended to the Republic for the first time in 50 years. The UDA was officially banned earlier in the year, but there was still no let-up on the C Company killing machine. By the end of 1992, 12 out of 19 UFF murders were civilians with no known connection to the IRA or Sinn Féin. These included the indiscriminate shooting of betting shops in Catholic areas, most notoriously the attack on 5 February when UFF killers shot dead five men including a 15-year old in Sean Graham's bookmakers on the Lower Ormeau Road in Belfast. Although those directly responsible came from the south and east Belfast UDA brigades, the unit involved were close associates of Adair. Indeed the man directly organising the massacre was on the UDA Inner Council with Adair. This act was executed with particular ruthlessness in large part because it was in retaliation, the UDA said, for the slaughter of eight Protestant workers at Teebane, Co. Tyrone, by the IRA. The Provos had targeted the men because they were working at a security force base in the county. Two images stand out from this particularly brutal period in the latter stages of the

Troubles. One was at Teebane Crossroads, where the entrails and human remains of the eight workers could be seen dangling from nearby trees after the huge bomb blast; the other was the sound of a horse race still running inside Sean Graham's a few weeks later as paramedics rushed to save survivors and bring out the dead in front of distraught relatives.

In February 1993 incendiary bombs were planted outside the homes of two Social Democratic and Labour Party (SDLP) councillors, marking a new escalation in the UDA's and specifically C Company's terror campaign. By the end of the first year, the overall terrorist death count had risen sharply and for the first time in the history of the modern Troubles the combined forces of the UDA/UFF and UVF were out-killing republicans. Between the two loyalist groups they had claimed 48 victims, most of them vulnerable Catholics, a smaller number Sinn Féin or IRA members; the IRA had killed 36 and the INLA had murdered two. The year 1993 would be the closest since the early 1970s that Northern Ireland teetered on the brink of civil war. That grim scenario was in large part due to the energy, callousness and murderous guile of Adair and his comrades in C Company.

By October 1993 the hostilities reached crisis point when ten people were killed by an IRA bomb at a fish shop on the Shankill Road. With the exception of one of the bombers who died at the scene, the remainder were Protestant civilians. The bombing signified the greatest loss of life in Northern Ireland in a single occurrence since the Enniskillen bombing on 8 November 1987. A further 57 people were injured in the attack. There was a wave of condemnations of the attack. Loyalist paramilitaries reacted immediately, shooting two Catholic men, one of whom died later from his wounds. Twelve Catholic civilians were killed within eight days of the bombing. Jackie was so incensed by the Shankill bomb that she personally offered to drive a car carrying an even bigger bomb to the Falls Road and return the destruction. However, her offer was rejected by the UDA as she was by then too well known. Adair and C Company planned a vengeance attack on 26 October at a bin depot at Kennedy Way in west Belfast. Two gunmen burst into the depot brandishing a handgun and a machine-gun and yelled, 'Take that, you bastards.' James Cameron, a 54-year-old road sweeper was killed and Mark Rodgers also lost his life as he attempted to crawl into the back of one of the bin trucks. Five more were wounded. According to Jackie, the operation was meant as a birthday offering for Johnny, who later commented that he was a 'wee bit disappointed' with the final body count.

Later that week, when Jackie was detained at Castlereagh Holding Centre, six more Catholic civilians and one Protestant were killed in a 'trick or treat' massacre at the Rising Sun Bar in Greysteel, Co. Derry/Londonderry. Another 13 people were injured and one later died of his injuries in April the following year. The attack was patent revenge for the Shankill Road bombing on 23 October. The killings brought the total number of deaths during October to 27.

'Johnny knew he was doing a lot of bad things but didn't know how to put it right because in his words, "There's a war on," says Jackie. 'After the IRA made a few attempts on his life, I remember him saying to me, "Jack, I don't want to die." I believe he still doesn't. Other people on the sideline, neighbours and others, only told me afterwards how terrified they were. I was on the Taughmonagh estate not long ago doing a woman's nails. Her boyfriend, who used to run around with my son years back, came in and he kept looking at me. "You were the one with the mad house," he said to me. I felt embarrassed and just sniggered a bit. It all seems so unreal now. My next door neighbour at the time, whom I met in Belfast one day not long ago, said, "I didn't have the heart to tell you, but I was afraid. You had everybody in there, all those high up ones. I was always afraid the IRA would come and get the wrong house." We had a laugh about it over a coffee, but I really didn't see the danger at the time. I didn't see my associates at that time as people who went out to kill other people. I'm truly amazed that nothing ever happened to me. I got into a taxi a year and a half ago and the guy said, "Good God, it's you! How are you?" He had been the milkman back then and his wife used to argue with him about me a lot because she didn't want him delivering milk to my house. She simply considered it too dangerous. If the IRA had really wanted to take out the top two dozen loyalist terrorists of that entire time, all they had to do was send a rocket launcher over to my house any Friday night. They had no idea how chaotically we lived.'

The events at one particular party in early 1993, however, are quite appalling, if only for the gullibility of the inadvertent victim involved. A well-heeled, affluent business woman from out of town—also a committed Christian and church-goer—got word that her daughter was dating one of Johnny's crew and was taking a lot of drugs. Distraught about her daughter being led astray and desperate to find out how the drugs were affecting her frame of mind, she tracked down some of the men at a nightclub in the area and asked them if she could buy an E. By the time she left Jackie's house, she would be deprived of her sanity, money, coat, car, and her knickers.

'The woman was too scared to come into my house. She had no idea who these men were but was feeling anxious,' remembers Jackie. 'Big Paul asked me to coax her in. "Go on, Jackie, tell her to come in. Tell her we're OK." The lads were impressed as she had a brand new car and was wearing an expensive new coat. I went out to the car and asked her if she'd come in. She said, "Ach no, I'm a bit afraid of them lot." I said, "Not at all, they're real nice men. They wouldn't do you any harm. Just come in for a wee while."

'The minute she hit the front door, they said, "Come on into the kitchen, love" and took her coat from her. They took £60 and gave her two aspirin, but then they gave her an E as well. After just 40 minutes or so she began losing the plot. They had been telling her that her daughter's boyfriend was a serial killer who dumped women's bodies in bins behind supermarkets across Northern Ireland and that he also specialised in killing policemen. She was beginning to get very freaked out. "No! He doesn't kill policemen," she kept saying. Then, all of a sudden, I saw her chasing him out of the kitchen and he was screaming, "Help me. Help. She's fucking nuts!" The Christian woman was sprinting after him with a huge carving knife, shouting, "I'm going to stab you." She was screaming the house down. I saw the shock on his face; he told me he was going with her daughter. The others were pissing themselves laughing. "Get him love, do away with that cop killer," they roared.

'They got the knife off her, but by this stage she was really going a bit plinky plonky. She was in the sitting room begging Big Donald to dance with her, getting down on her hands and knees telling him, "Please, they're going to kill me." I said to one of the other guys, "C'mon and we'll wind these ones up here", meaning the boyfriend and this woman. So they took him up to one of the bedrooms and told him they had received information he was working for Special Branch and to take his clothes off. He fell for it immediately. "I'm not lads, I swear I'm not!" We got him to look out the window and showed him some parked cars and said, "There are Special Branch people out there watching this place, and you brought them here." Then we stripped him down.

There was a huge commotion on the landing. At this stage the woman was losing it. She ran into the bathroom but slipped and fell on the floor knocking herself out. One of the lads grabbed her, stuck her head down the toilet and flushed it. Then another one, off his head on drugs, ran up the stairs, grabbed her and threw her on the bed. That's when they saw she had no knickers on. The driver had apparently shagged her on the way up in her car. They were joking about, saying, "Who wants to have a go at her?" But I put an end to that as it was abusive.

'When she came around, she had obviously no idea why she was on the bed and turned nasty. "I want to leave," she said. She went to go down the stairs but again one of the lads pulled up her skirt and said, "Give us a look at that hairy thing, will ye?" She flung herself around and boxed my niece in the face. I jumped up. "Don't lift your fucking hand to her. She didn't touch you." My niece hit her and the woman went to hit her again. I knocked her down and jumped on her head a bit. It started to get completely out of hand. I said to the lads, "Get her out of this house now or I'll kill her." I meant it.

'She was kneeling on the floor praying to God to save her. They realised I was really serious so they took her out. In the meantime, they had taken a meat fork out of my drawer and burst her tyres. She put her coat on. There were no sleeves on it. They had cut them off, and Fuzzy shit in the pocket. The boyfriend put it on after they had done a job on it, putting his hand in the pocket, but he was so off his head he thought the shit was blood and was screaming about someone being murdered. They got her into the car, drove her to a garage to get it sorted, and left her there. All you could hear was the thump thump thump of the car wheels slowly edging their way out of the estate. Before she left they took another £60 off her for more Anadin and rang her daughter. "We've just shagged your fucking mother, the auld dog in the fancy coat. She was rightly up for it. She's on her way back to you off her head on drugs. Make sure now she gets a good night's sleep."'

03 | SOMEONE LOVES BASEBALL

*The subject was told to sort herself out and tell us the truth.
She remained silent. We discussed the evils of terrorism and
asked her to dissociate herself from the UFF. We asked her
why she was adopting the attitude of a hardened terrorist.
We then went on to ask her if she thought it was a proper
way to bring up her children with murderers hanging
around her home. Again, she made no reply.*

The cold metal bed base and biscuit-thin mattress in the 6 m x 2 drab cell was all the reality check Jackie needed as she gracelessly changed into a white boiler suit before being led away for an inaugural interrogation. With zero natural lighting and even less heat, it was obvious the facilities here were not up to much. Jackie glared at the female officer who had just told her, smirking, that her children were going to be taken away from her for good. 'Are you taking the piss out of me?' she snapped. She realised that her uniform for the next few days was at least four sizes too big. 'Don't worry, love, no one here cares what you look like,' the officer said. 'It's not what's *on* you, but what's *in* you that concerns us.'

The image of her children crying dominated her thoughts inside the near-empty room. She had heard plenty of daunting tales of what they put you through in loyalist publications and first-hand accounts from friends. Hard men involved in terrible crimes were known to crumble under the mental pressure after just a few days. One man she knew confessed to a murder that would later be proven in court he could not have had anything to do with. Another man on the Taughmonagh estate, according to Jackie, served ten years for a terrorist-related crime he did not commit. He told her that the psychological mind games had proved too much. He regretted signing a confession, but when they said they were going to lift his wife, who was very ill at the time, he had floundered. What could possibly make a person weaken to the extent where they would prefer a lengthy prison sentence to a few days of questioning?

'It was in my mind right from the beginning that the best way to get through it was to pick a spot on the wall and keep staring at it,' says Jackie. 'There were only two things on my mind, my son and my daughter. That's all I cared about; Johnny Adair couldn't have been further from my mind. You could buy these wee magazines at the time, published by the UDA, with stories from prisoners as well as general news. I remember reading prisoners' accounts of Castlereagh and the mental pressure that the process puts on you. I knew I had to be very strong-minded in order to survive days of grilling about information that I simply didn't have to give.'

—

Allegations of torture, beatings and human rights abuses had been rife at Castlereagh since the very beginning of the Troubles. When the centre opened in the early 1970s, it struck fear into the hearts of toughened loyalist and republican activists alike. Ironically, the Royal Ulster Constabulary's (RUC) interrogation techniques at Castlereagh would subsequently change the way terrorists operated, opting instead for more interdependent terror cells with only scant information concerning operations being passed on between individuals. This would, with a bit of luck, counteract the possibility of detainees 'breaking' and passing on information to the police about murders, bombings and other terrorist deeds. Such was the centre's reputation for victory over the malevolence of terrorism that during one three-year period in the 1970s, more than 3,000 people were charged with terrorist offences. The majority of confessions were obtained at Castlereagh. Its success rate in 'getting people to talk' became renowned across the world.

Undoubtedly the techniques of Castlereagh resulted in the supergrass system of the early 1980s, when several hardcore republican and loyalist terrorists broke down, confessed and then agreed, in order to get lighter sentences, to turn Queen's evidence against their comrades. Although the supergrass system was later discredited in the late 1980s through a series of landmark judicial rulings in Belfast, it could be argued that its by-product was to sow suspicion, doubt and fear inside terrorist groups. For instance, the already volatile INLA fell apart in the late 1980s in large part due to the supergrass system. Such was the paranoia within the INLA prisoners locked up inside the Victorian Crumlin Road Jail in Belfast, that faction fighting broke out among the inmates. These internal battles were merely a precursor to the deadly feuds that tore the INLA asunder in 1987–88. A similar situation was generated within all the other paramilitary organisations in the North, and to an extent the interrogation crafts honed in Castlereagh played a part in generating that paranoia.

However, there was also a litany of serious setbacks for the RUC throughout the centre's contentious career. In May 1978 suspect Brian Maguire, who was being questioned about a murder, hanged himself in his Castlereagh cell. According to *An Phoblacht*, a republican newspaper, a UDA man who was held in the cell opposite Brian Maguire reported that RUC detectives asked him what he thought of their 'handiwork', referring to Maguire's death. His death resulted in the Bennett Inquiry, a three-man committee lead by Crown Court judge Harry Bennett and it was agreed in its aftermath that CCTVs must be installed in interview rooms and detainees allowed access to a solicitor after 48 hours. Police doctor Robert Irwin made a statement to the Bennett Inquiry to the effect that he had recorded no less than 150 cases of injuries inflicted on prisoners during police interrogation in Castlereagh and other police barracks in

Northern Ireland. The methods of interrogation studied by the Bennett report intimate that without the ability of the police to obtain confessions, the entire justice system of the time would have buckled. At the time, more than 94 per cent of terrorist-related cases heard at the Belfast City Commission (the special courts) resulted in a conviction. Of these the prosecution in between 75–80 per cent of cases depended almost completely on statements made by those detained at Castlereagh.

Allegations of beatings and abuse plummeted after the inquiry but never entirely disappeared. In the early years accusations centred around many physical methods the RUC allegedly used: beatings, twisting limbs, applying pressure to sensitive points on the body, drawn out periods of standing or squatting in awkward positions, prolonged physical exercises, burning with cigarettes, and even attempted strangulation, according to individual accounts. Mental pressures alleged included prolonged oppressive questioning, threats of imprisonment, threats to the family of the suspect, stripping, and verbal abuse and humiliation.

The RUC's response to those allegations in the 1970s was that it was little more than deliberate propaganda that would hopefully reduce police effectiveness against paramilitary groups. It argued that detainees often mutilated themselves before making official complaints. In June 1977, the then Chief Constable Kenneth Leslie Newman issued a statement saying that some detainees had clearly tried to cause self harm by 'eating utensils, a nail, a tin of lemonade, or by butting their head against a wall or smashing a window'. While there may well be strands of truth in the counter-allegations, grievances of ill-treatment continued on into the 1980s and 90s. Both Amnesty International and Helsinki Watch, an international human rights watchdog established in 1978, made quite a few impassioned pleas to have the centre shut down. In 1994, one year after Jackie's detention, QC Sir Louis Blom-Cooper, appointed by the Secretary of State to oversee holding centres, called for its closure. The matter was continually raised during meetings of the Anglo-Irish Conference and the closure of Castlereagh was one of the major demands of Sinn Féin in its submission to Patten.

A defining moment on the issue of Castlereagh came after the 1991 case of Damien Austin, a 17-year-old west Belfast youth who alleged detectives hacked out stitches in his ear, pressed a cigarette lighter to his testicles and punched him persistently during his detention. Austin's case was particularly controversial as his alleged brutal treatment was apparently connected to the killing of an RUC officer in an IRA rocket attack on 1 May 1991. He later told Helsinki Watch: 'They punched me and kicked me and beat me every day. One of them spat in my face. They kept telling me they would kill me. I was made stand in the middle of the room as they walked behind me and slapped me real hard on the back of my head. They told me all my friends had signed statements and that I was going to jail. They threatened to take me to a loyalist area and leave me there. They said I'd be dead before Christmas.'

Damien was released without any charges on 10 May and arrested again on 17 August 1991. 'I saw a doctor in Castlereagh at about 8 a.m. The doctor said there were no marks on my body, but that I had four stitches in my right ear. From 8.30 until 1 p.m. I was questioned by six detectives, working two at a time. It was a hundred times worse than what happened to me on 7 May. They hit me under the chin, and in my stomach, and on my arms and my throat and on the back of my head. At one point I collapsed, and they lifted me up and hit me again. They had me in a choke hold and I couldn't breathe. I had two other questioning sessions that day. They made me stand for long times, once for about four hours. And in the afternoon interview somebody pulled my head backwards over the chair and held it there for a long time. They gave me dinner, and then they questioned me again from 7.30 p.m. until midnight. They hit me and punched me again, and one detective put his boot between my legs and pushed my testicles. One detective held me around the neck in an arm lock; I thought I was going to pass out. I kept asking to see a doctor, but they wouldn't let me. On Sunday at 7.30 a.m. I saw the doctor and he saw bruises and told me he would go to court and testify for me. He gave me two asthma inhalers and pain killers. The detectives wouldn't let me use the inhalers during the interviews, even

though they knew I had asthma. They did the same things to me on Sunday that they had on Saturday. Then a new detective came in before dinner time and said, "I'm going to kill you. I'm going to make you a living shell." Then he grabbed my ears and pulled them. The cut that I had on my right ear started bleeding, and two of the stitches were pulled out. Blood dripped on to my T-shirt. After dinner they squeezed my testicles again. The detective was sitting on the back of a chair in front of me. After the detectives left, I saw blood on my trousers. There was blood on my face, too; one of the detectives said they wouldn't talk to me when I had blood on my face, and spat on a dirty handkerchief and wiped my face with it. Later they took me back to my cell, and when I took off my trousers, I saw blood on my under shorts, and I could see that it had come from my penis. On Monday morning I saw the doctor again, and he saw marks and bruises on me. Then they interviewed me again and kept hitting me like they had done before. I saw my solicitor at about 10.30 a.m. and he told me to ask to see my own doctor. The beatings got worse after this.'
Damien also claimed that officers said they would give the UVF information on him and his family before releasing him finally without charge. He later received compensation from the British government for his ordeal.

Another highly publicised case was that of David Adams, who claimed officers at the centre broke his leg during interrogation. He also stated that his face was scraped along the ground, that he was kicked, punched, and beaten on the head and back with weapons. Adams, who is a cousin of Sinn Féin president Gerry Adams, spent a total of three weeks in hospital after his ordeal, where he also received treatment for a punctured right lung, fractured ribs and injuries to the forehead, nose, lower lip and chin and his right eye. He was eventually awarded £30,000 in 1998 in a civil action against RUC officers at the centre. (It is worth noting here that Adams was arrested on an IRA mission to assassinate RUC Superintendent Derek Martindale. Ironically, it was Martindale who was one of the detectives later to interview Adams about the assault by fellow RUC officers.)

When operational, Castlereagh Holding Centre was basically a bundle of prefabricated buildings within the confines of Castlereagh Police Station in east Belfast. There were 31 cells in the building—four located in a distinct section for women detainees. There were also 21 interview rooms, two further rooms for consultations with solicitors, a doctor's surgery and a 'scenes of crime' unit. The interview rooms were divided between one set of 13 bordering on the cells, and another set of eight in an unconnected building. Inside each was a scrubby mix of a table, three chairs and two wall-mounted cameras. On the outside of the main interview block the windows were covered with plywood, apart from one section of each which had been fitted with a cowl, allowing some fresh air but no natural light to enter the cells and rooms. This was apparently necessary for security reasons.

—

On the day of her arrest Jackie had a sense of foreboding that something extraordinary was about to happen. 'That day we had planned a shopping trip to town and I was looking forward to buzzing around a few shopping centres and maybe having a bite to eat in one of the cafés. But all I could hear was the hum of a helicopter and Land Rovers piling into the estate earlier that morning.'

The Land Rovers backed right up to her front door while uniformed personnel broke down the front and back door of her Taughmonagh council house. Jackie, who was upstairs in her bedroom with her daughter, son and John Crockard and two nieces, ran down the stairs to see what the commotion was about. Thunderous roars greeted her: 'Get into the living room now. Don't move. No one move.' The entire estate had been cordoned off; no one could get in or out. Neighbours stood in astonishment at their hall doors; some jammed their faces against sitting room windows to gaze at the bedlam outside; others flustered about, unnerved, making sure their children were safe indoors. This was a well-organised raid just one day after the Kennedy Way murders. The RUC was adamant that Jackie could have made the initial call to Model Taxis in Belfast for a car that was consequently hijacked and used in the butchery by the UFF.

On this day, too, a debate was taking place in Seanad Éireann, the upper house of the Irish Parliament, about the ongoing spate of killings in the North with particular reference to the Shankill bombing and the Kennedy Way murders in late autumn 1993. Senator McGowan opened by saying: 'There was hope that we could resolve our political differences within the context of a European Common Market, but there is still an element that has no patience and who seem to thrive on using the gun and slaughtering innocent people. That behaviour is alien to the vast majority of the Irish people. Whether you come from the Shankill or elsewhere, killing human beings will not solve the problem.' Senator Manning responded: 'There is a very dark cloud of despair hanging over the whole island and in particular over the northern part. I do not believe there has been a time in the last 25 years when people have felt so fearful, helpless and hopeless in the face of the terrible events of the past couple of days.'

The previous Saturday, 23 October 1993, was another run-of-the-mill shopper's afternoon, when the Shankill without warning became a scene of blood and carnage when a bomb exploded in Frizzell's fish shop. Ten people were killed including one of the IRA bombers, Thomas 'Bootsy' Begley, when the 11-second timed mechanical escape pact botched and the bomb exploded prematurely. The other bomber, Sean Kelly, survived and was later jailed for the attack, receiving nine life sentences, but was later released under the Good Friday Agreement in 2000.

Jackie was driving through east Belfast with her daughter when she heard the loud bang. 'I noticed a lot of fellas running up the road and getting into their cars,' says Jackie. 'My daughter and John had gone into the chippy for something to eat when he ran out and over to the car, "Johnny's been killed! They've done the UDA headquarters." My mind was immediately in a spin. It couldn't be true. I prayed to God with all my might that Johnny was still alive. When we got to the bottom of the Shankill the whole road had been shut off. We started to walk towards the fish shop. When we got past Agnes Street there were people running everywhere in a total panic, shouting and screaming. I knew then it was bad. They were making human chains to get rid of rubble outside the shop itself. I looked around for a familiar face and saw Joe Bratty with Bubbles and a load of UDA men from the south. They told me Johnny had left an hour before for Magilligan Prison in Limavady and was safe. It was hard to take in the scene. A man from Berlin Street told me afterwards how he lifted up a human foot that was stuck to a piece of rubble. The police had by this stage moved in with heat-seeking devices and told some men to move as they were, unbeknownst to them, sitting on a woman who was still alive. Apparently three civilians who were helping to dig people out of the rubble actually lifted Sean Kelly up, still very much alive, and wondered why he was wearing surgical gloves. He shared an ambulance with a young man who was badly injured. Even in the dreadfully wounded state he was in, he made a run for it, or at least tried to.

Like many on the Shankill and far beyond, Jackie wanted revenge. 'We heard stories later on from people at the scene that they pulled one man out who blinked and asked if he was still alive. He was so happy to know he had made it, but he actually died before they put him in the ambulance. That story summed up the horror for me. I knew Johnny too felt sick to the stomach and guilt-ridden because he said to me later that night on the phone, "Jack, that bomb was meant for me." I was so incredibly sickened by the whole thing that the minute I went back to the estate, I rang Alec Kerr and told him straight out to put a massive bomb in the boot of my car and I'd drive up to the Falls Road or into Ardoyne and let them [Catholics] have it. I would have done that, no problem, without a second thought, I was so enraged, but Alec said I was too well known by then. At the end of the day paramilitaries are an army; they believe in what they are fighting for, and I too believed there were legitimate targets, but not innocent people, not the likes of ordinary people out doing their shopping. That's really sick. I would have done anything at that moment to settle the score; that's how a lot of loyalists felt in the wake of the bomb. "These were innocent people, Jack," Adair declared. "There's no need for innocents to lose their lives like

that, no need at all." I knew Johnny wouldn't let the IRA away with
it. He was deeply affected by the bombing and I admired him for
that.'

The IRA's intended target was undoubtedly Johnny Adair
himself, who used the space above the shop to hold cloak-and-
dagger UFF meetings. The bombing prompted a wave of reprisals.
The UVF immediately killed two innocent Catholic men, and later
on in the week the UFF attacked a bar in Greysteel, killing a
further seven people. Stephen Irwin, just 20 years old at the time,
was convicted and given eight life sentences for the murder, along
with three other UFF men. Later released from Long Kesh in July
2000, he was remanded once again after stabbing a football
supporter with a knife during the 2004 Irish cup final. October
1993 was dubbed the most vicious and violent month in 17 years
and it seemed the UFF were teeming with belligerent young
recruits intent on maintaining the war with the IRA.

It was only days later that Jackie was 'lifted' and taken to
Castlereagh and she was still reeling with anger, even though the
UFF crusade of vengeance had already claimed a number of lives.
Her first reaction was to roar abuse at the RUC officers ransacking
her home. 'I was shouting out the window and the police were
going completely mad,' she recalls. 'One of them kept signalling
to a female officer, saying, "Get her away from the window!" and
I was shouting back, "Fuck off, you bastards! What kind of
wankers are you?" They ran around like parasites up the stairs,
into the kitchen, out into the back garden. They were taking
swabs from the wallpaper, emptying out bins for evidence; there
was a full forensic squad tearing my house to bits. We were told
to sit down while they searched. "Was your boyfriend here last
night?" one of them bawled, but I just replied, "I don't know what
you're talking about." They had obviously been watching Johnny
all along, so why weren't they lifting him? What the hell could I
tell them? He had left my house at about 8 a.m. They emptied the
wheelie bin and put everything in plastic bags; it was obviously a
scare tactic. Why they wanted rubbish from the bin was beyond
me. We continued calling them wankers and the female officers
lesbians. One of the women was particularly ugly, butch and

dykey looking, like a Nazi female. I turned to one of the detectives and teased him, "You're gorgeous you are, you're just like superman, but she's an awful ugly looking cow, isn't she?" My kids just sat there staring; they weren't a bit freaked out. They brought me into the kitchen and a brown bag was sitting on the floor. They said to me, "Jacqueline Robinson, you are the householder?" I said, "Well, it's kind of looking that way, isn't it?" They then informed me that I was being arrested under Section 34 of the Terrorism Act.

"'There's a brown bag there and in it there's baseball bats, some caps and gloves. What does that tell you?" one of them asked. I responded, "Someone loves baseball?" They were not impressed by that at all. I kept looking at the bag; I genuinely didn't know whose it was. I hadn't seen it before. It turns out it belonged to John Crockard. To me there was nothing in it to indicate paramilitary activity, like masks, for instance. They had found it in the garden hedges; John had thrown it there, so he was eventually nabbed as well. It was just the excuse they needed to arrest me. I don't know what they would have done otherwise. They also accused me there and then of doing "their" washing after the Kennedy Way shootings; they thought I was burning evidence on the open fire. They kept saying that I allowed paramilitaries to conduct meetings at my house and they told me I'd "go down" for it. At this stage the kids started getting upset.

'I went into the sitting room and John said to me, "Three days, Jackie, that's all they'll keep you for. Chin up, you'll get through it." My daughter started to get hysterical, lifted the coal bucket and flung it at a police woman as she led me out. "Take that, you bitch. Leave my mother alone!" It was very emotional. As I was being led out, there was a police woman in front and a man behind me to make sure I couldn't escape, as if I could. As they put me in the back seat of a red Sierra, I could hear my children crying. I didn't have time to say goodbye to them. I just sat in the car as it sped off towards Castlereagh Holding Centre. All I could think of was, "Jesus, those sirens are going a bit mad." My life seemed to come to a swift halt.

'When the gates opened and we sped through, there were

police wagons and cars everywhere. My heart really started to thump. I had a panic attack and asked to speak to my kids. The police woman said, "We'll see what we can do." Her whole attitude changed towards me in that car and I knew she was trying to soft-soap me. She knew I was worried about my kids and that might have been a way to get the information they wanted. After sitting in the car for about ten minutes, they then took me into this hut where I had to take off all my jewellery and put it in a bag. They took me down a long corridor and into the bottom cell. Three or four more came along then and they told me to take all my clothes off. The police woman stood as I undressed. I began to feel a bit stronger. An hour later they took my photograph and put me back in the cell. Then the doctor came and asked me some questions to see if I was mentally stable and able for interrogation. The questions were a bit ridiculous really—"Are you feeling stressed?" I was a wee bit nervous because I didn't know what to expect. Two officers then came along and took me to another prefab with a few rooms. I was taken into the first room and I could hear what was going on in the room next to me. There was a girl in there very upset. I found out later she was accused of making a phone call to a taxi company whose car was hijacked for the Kennedy Way murders, although they were also trying to pin that on me. Her mother was with her as she was a minor. I could hear her screaming and weeping; she was really howling. That made me terribly nervous. They waited until her 18th birthday, which was two weeks after, and lifted her then. She owned up to making the phone call to the taxi rank to come to Carlisle Circus where the Kennedy Way shooters hijacked the taxi.

'A female officer came into the room. She was very attractive. She told me her name. Another man 'X' was also there who was very well known, a fat bastard about whom I would later make a complaint as he was always drunk. You could smell the alcohol off him all the time. The female detective said to me, "Jackie, do you know Johnny Adair?" I said "No." "Really? We find that hard to believe because you've been fucking him for the last nine months." She flung a file a mile high in front of me. It was chocka-block with all kinds of detail: who had gone in and out of my house; at what times; my comings and goings and my kids'. I knew we were under surveillance because the police were always outside my house, but it was bizarre to see the file.

'She said to me, "We've got a file on you, as you can see, with every detail; in fact the person you thought was the plumber across the road was staking out your house all the time. You wouldn't have known. Even the person you were sitting next to on the bus might have been watching you for us." She was right, of course; that's how they did their surveillance. I was then cautioned and the first interrogation was under way.'

Q. Can you give us an account of your movements on Monday, 25 October 1993?

A. I went to work in a building beside the Ulster Hall. I have a cleaning job there to tide me over till Christmas.

Q. What time did you leave home?

A. About 4.30. I got a bus down.

Q. What time did you arrive home again?

A. About ten to seven/seven o'clock.

Q. Who was in your house when you got home?

A. My son and daughter.

Q. Anyone else?

A. My sister's two kids.

Q. Were there any callers to your house on Monday night, that's two nights ago now?

A. No, I just went to my sister's house for an hour or so.

Q. What ages are your son and daughter?

A. 16 and 13.

Q. Did you speak to anyone else that night?

A. No, just my sister.

Q. Where does she live?

A. 10 Finch Way.

Q. What is her name?

A. Kim Thomason.

Q. Can you remember if you made any phone calls?

A. I think I may have phoned a girl I work with.

Q. Who is she?

A. Eileen. She lives in the estate.

Q. Did you receive any phone calls?

A. Not on Monday night, none that I can recall.

Q. Are you sure about the time you were out of the house on Monday night?

A. Yes.

Q. Any possibility that you could have called later at her house?

A. No, her kids are young; she puts them to bed around 8 o'clock.

Q. Are you positive you didn't receive any telephone calls yourself before you went out?

A. Yes.

Q. Do you know any people who live on the Shankill Road?

A. I know some people but I don't know any addresses of people.

Q. Where do you socialise?

A. Just in the Taughmonagh Club. I go with my sister and a friend.

Q. Who is she?

A. Julie. I don't bother with people from outside the estate.

Q. Do you know anyone who works in the shipyard?

A. No.

Q. Do you know a street called Southpark Court?

A. I've never heard of it. I'm from the village.

Q. Do you use taxis much?

A. If I'm going down the town on Saturday night or to B&Q during the day.

Q. What taxis would you use?

A. A local firm.

Q. Did you ever use a taxi from Model Taxis?

A. Never heard of it. Where's it from?

Q. Did you ever use a taxi to go over to the Shankill?

A. At a do in the Diamond Bar. It was the only time I socialised on the Shankill.

Q. On Monday night past would you have any cause to order

a taxi?

A. No, I wasn't out so I had no need to order a taxi.

Q. Did anyone ask you on Monday night to order a taxi for them?

A. No, there was nobody about.

Q. Was your daughter's boyfriend in the house on Monday night?

A. No, he wasn't.

Q. What is his name?

A. John.

Q. Where is he from?

A. Finaghy. I don't know the address.

Q. Did he stay in your house last night?

A. Yes, that's why he was there this morning.

Q. What time did he arrive at last night?

A. It was yesterday morning, sometime between 11 o'clock and one o'clock.

Q. Was John in your house all day?

A. Yes, he and my daughter took my son to Funderland around half past seven.

Q. What time did they come home at?

A. About 10.

Q. When John stays in your house overnight, where does he sleep?

A. In my son's room and my son sleeps in with me.

Q. Did John bring an overnight bag with him?

A. No.

Q. Did he bring an overnight bag yesterday?

A. No.

Q. How frequently would he stay overnight in your house?

A. Maybe once or twice a week.

Q. Did he stay in your house on Monday night?

A. Yes, he did.

Q. What time did he arrive at?

A. I can't remember. I'm no good at remembering times.

Q. What time did he leave yesterday?

A. About 9 or 10 I suppose.

Q. Apart from John, can you tell us the last male visitor to your house?

A. None.

Q. Have you a boyfriend that visits your house?

A. No, I haven't got a boyfriend.

Q. Do you know a person called Johnny Adair?

A. I know of him.

Q. How do you know him?

A. Through the club; everybody heads down there at weekends.

Q. Did you meet Johnny Adair at the club?

A. I didn't meet him as such. I just said hello, the way I do with everyone else.

Q. Have you ever brought a male friend back to your house?

A. No, not in front of the children. They are at an impressionable age.

Q. Who else have you brought into your house, male persons that is?

A. None. I socialise in the club or at my sister's or in the Elbow Room on a Saturday night.

Q. When did the painters arrive at your house?

A. This morning, just about an hour before your people came.

Q. The bag that was shown to you at your house this morning was found in your back garden.

A. I know nothing about it.

Q. We have reason to believe that John threw it away when he ran from the back of your house.

A. I don't know.

Q. John ran out of your house. Didn't you know?

A. No, I didn't. He came down the stairs after me when I went to answer the door to you.

Q. Do you own this bag?

A. No.

Q. This bag contained terrorist-type articles. How did they get into your house?

A. I don't know. I have explained everything to you.

Q. Have you ever seen this bag before?

A. No.

Q. Can we take it that you have never handled anything in this bag?

A. No, I have not.

Q. When were you last in your back garden?

A. I was out getting coal and at my wheelie bin yesterday.

Q. What time would that have been?

A. I don't know.

Q. Did you see this bag in your garden then?

A. No, I didn't.

Q. Do you accept that this bag found in your back garden and shown to you was in your kitchen this morning, and that it contained three baseball caps, two pairs of gloves, three scarves, a black nylon holdall and a starting pistol?

A. I'm not accepting anything until I see it.

Q. The articles will be shown to you in due course.

'I started to learn quite quickly what their tactics entailed,' says Jackie. 'That first interview was fine, really mild, but each one just got worse and worse. They were giving out about a friend of ours, John, saying he was a murdering bastard etc. and that he was with my daughter, that it must run in the family, this addiction to terrorists. They also said he was having sex with my daughter and they would have him done for unlawful carnal knowledge as the legal age for sex is 17 in Northern Ireland. Then they started to play serious mind games telling me they had been in touch with social services and they had already taken my kids. I didn't know whether to believe them or not; instinctively I felt they were telling lies, but when you're in that situation your mind can play tricks and you start to believe them even after an hour or so. They were drumming it into my head that I was going to lose my kids. That interview didn't last too long, about an hour. They took me back to the cell and offered me something to eat, but I refused it. I'd heard about them spitting and pissing in the food, and worse, picking their noses and doing all sorts of grotesque things, so I wouldn't eat a thing the whole time I was in there, not a solitary bite. They brought me in a cup of tea. That is all I would accept.'

The noises filtering through from the surrounding cells did nothing to ease Jackie's tension. 'I could hear a voice I recognised, a woman; it turned out to be Rosie, a girl from the Shankill. Her husband had been done for having rocket launchers in his back garden and they had lifted her to put pressure on him. Every time I heard them walking down and putting the key in her cell door I kept thinking, I wish they'd come to me and not her, because she was really hysterical. I found listening to that more upsetting than going through it myself. They were giving her a real bad time. I could hear her screaming, 'Please, no, it wasn't me. . . .' They were doing a right job on her. But the idea is that you hear other people's situations as well. Men find it hard to cope with and they didn't ease up on the women either. And because I was Johnny's so-called partner at the time, they put that supplementary pressure on me. Cathy Spruce had been lifted before and squealed on Johnny, so I presume they thought I'd be an easy source for information as well. And on top of that I had kids, so they could really put me under pressure. Something told me I had to be strong. There was always a man and a woman, and just like the movies they'd play the good cop, bad cop thing. The guy would say, "C'mon now, Jackie, I tell ye what it is. You tell us what's happened. Who's going to know? We won't say that you said. . . ." And I'm thinking, Fuck off, you stupid bastard. Do you think I'm daft? He'd keep saying to me, "Jackie, you know Johnny Adair preys on women like you, single women, vulnerable women; he does that all the time. You're not his only girlfriend; he has buckets of them. You don't need to be involved in all this. You've got a nice home. Tell us how you can afford it." They had me convinced before the end of the first day that no matter what, I was going to prison.'

Cross-examinations were scheduled every hour and a half with an hour's break in between. As time went on each interview became more difficult and heavy-handed. At 19.33 on the first night, she was asked straight out if she was a leading member of the UFF.

A. No, I'm fucking not.

Q. Do you know if John, your daughter's friend, is in the UFF?

A. He's a nice quiet lad.

Q. What do you know about the find of two shotguns wrapped in a towel and inside clear plastic bin bags?

A. I know sweet fuck all.

Q. Has Johnny Adair ever been in your home?

A. No.

Q. When did you last see him?

A. About seven or eight months ago.

Q. Where?

A. I gave him a lift from the Kimberley Bar with a few other people and took them to Taughmonagh Club.

'We told Robinson to sort herself out. She stated that she had nothing more to tell us and was innocent. We told her that we didn't believe her and we would be returning her to her cell to have a think about her position.'

'My head started to go boogaloo when I was in the cell alone in between the interviews,' Jackie recollects. 'I was sitting there thinking, what the hell am I going to do? What about my kids? I was really upset about my children. I was thinking they must be going crazy and kept imagining them in the care of social services, like I had been as a child. I didn't cry though; I never let them see me upset, because I knew they would close in on me even more. I didn't let them get to me. They just kept coming back, hoping I'd get weaker and weaker. To top it all off, I simply refused to eat. I was getting enough shit off them as it was without having to eat shit in a sandwich, which is what I heard they liked to dish up as a main course, the dirty bastards. The cell door kept opening every hour or so, it seemed. I dreaded it but I willed it to happen too because the more it did, the sooner I'd be home with my children. "Come with us," they'd say, one leading the way in front, another doddering behind. They changed rooms all the time as well, so that nothing became familiar and nothing was customary or relaxed. Sometimes we went upstairs. "Turn to the right now" and they'd also change officers on the way, I guess to make it a more chilly procedure. I'm sure this was to disorientate me.

'There was an older woman who was so well versed at playing mind games it was almost like being at the theatre. "C'mon now, you're a nice person. I know you are, Jackie. Don't fall into this trap that these murderers have set for you. Do you think for one second they care about you?" They brought up the topic of the taxi thing all the time, saying that I made phone calls to taxi firms for other murders and for the murder the minor was later done for. "You made that call to Model Taxis to call to Carlisle Circus and we know the car was then hijacked and used in the murder. Do you know Carlisle Circus, Jackie?" I'd reply, "No, don't know it", but of course I did. I didn't answer in the affirmative to anything as I was afraid they would twist the whole thing and bang me up quick."

On the second day Jackie reverted to shush mode and let them get annoyed instead.

Q. Have you been told about two shotguns found at the rear of your house on ground close by?

A. No reply.

Q. What made you become involved with paramilitaries, Jackie?

A. No reply.

Q. These guns and articles found in the holdall in your back garden are presently being examined by forensic scientists. Have you handled any of these articles?

A. No reply.

Q. We believe you phoned Model Taxis on Monday night to arrange a cab to be used in the murders the next day.

A. No reply.

Q. We know that Johnny Adair calls to your house frequently. Why do you continuously deny him even being in your house?

A. No reply.

Q. Do you deny being involved with the UFF?

A. I told you yesterday, I know nothing about them.

'I cried when I eventually saw details of the Kennedy Way murders, those bin men, after my release,' admits Jackie. 'I couldn't understand why they were trying to pin any part of this on me. I didn't know about it until I got out of there later that week. It had just happened the night before, on Johnny's birthday, but I learnt later that it was a "birthday present" for him. A top loyalist told me that. They would go over the same questions again and again. They rely on you going crazy; I could see how it could happen. So this went on all day, but on the second day it was relentless. I would have only just settled in the cell when they would come for me again, so I was getting more tired with each interrogation. I still hadn't eaten, but I did perk up; I felt much stronger mentally. You have to make a conscious decision at some point to either allow yourself to be broken down or to fight like a giant. The solicitor would be along soon and that made me feel a wee bit more secure. In the meantime their line of questions served only to give me an insight into what they wanted to know, so when my solicitor did eventually arrive, I told him what they were looking for. I turned it into a useful tool for myself. I had made my mind up by the second day to fuck them up completely.

'By the afternoon of day two my mindset had changed. The only person that can put me away without forensic evidence was myself. I had nothing to hide whatsoever. I had had no part in anything, so I had to keep reminding myself of that fact. No matter what they said to me, I didn't flinch. "We know you've been doing their washing; we know you've been helping these people out; we know you've been having UDA meetings in your house; we know you're a part of this." They even accused me of being a top UFF woman. They said, "How did you move across to Northern Ireland from the UK and become a top UFF woman so quickly?" I retorted, "What the fuck are you talking about, you fat bastard?"

'To be honest, though, I was feeling a bit scared. The incidents they mentioned were quite serious. They kept telling me about things Johnny was supposed to have done. "How could you get yourself involved with a man who kills people?" I would say, "I don't know anything about it. I don't know that man you are referring to. I don't know anyone who kills." But they kept on, "We know different, Jackie. We know different." At one point they handed me pen and paper and asked me to name a price: "Write down there what sum of money you consider to be fair and we'll take it from there." Journalists would later say that I was offered £1 million, but that's totally wrong. There was no actual price named because I never wrote anything on that piece of paper. They said, "We'll move all your stuff. You'll get to go anywhere in the world, you and your kids, and we'll protect you." I told them where to go with their money. They didn't like that at all. "I'm not getting a bullet in the back of the head for you bastards."

—

'Interview was delayed as subject had asked for a solicitor at 11.20 a.m. After police had contacted her solicitor's office we then told her that we were continuing our enquiries into her involvement with the UDA/UFF for the past number of months. It was put to her that she is believed to have made a phone call in relation to the Kennedy Way murders. She stated that she wasn't answering any questions. It was put to her that her house is a safe house for all the leading UFF murderers. It had been put to her that Johnny Adair was in her house—it was now known that he was in the house on many occasions and she wasn't denying this. She was asked if she knew of the seriousness of her position. It was pointed out that Johnny Adair and Joe Bratty were two men who had been using her home regularly; both had been targets for assassination by the PIRA on six occasions each to date. It was clear that they were using her home and had these weapons about in close proximity in case of attack. She was continuously questioned about who brought the weapons to her home. She refused to answer any questions. She was asked if she was frightened of these people and if she was acting under duress by keeping their gear for them. She again refused to answer. It was put to her that a party in her house on 18 October 1993 was for the leading members of the UFF and she consented to them using her house as she is part and parcel of the set-up. It was put to her that she was even letting them use her car. We continued to question her about her involvement with the UFF but she refused to answer any questions.'

A day later, notes from the cross-examination carried on with the same rhythmic theme: 'She sat with her arms folded looking straight ahead and refused to answer any questions. It was put to her that when the police arrived at her home and she answered the door, Crockard came down the stairs behind her wearing purple boxer shorts. She was asked why he came down the stairs with her. She refused to answer. It was put to her that this being the situation, Crockard wouldn't have had time to make his exit out the rear, jump over the fence at numbers 8 or 9 and then make his way back to her house again without the police, who entered from the front of the house, seeing him. She refused to answer any questions. She was asked if her daughter had got engaged to this man. She refused to answer. She was then shown the items that were found on her property. She made no reply. We then told her she showed all the hallmarks of a hardened terrorist. She sat on the chair yawning and made no reply. We spoke to her about her habits of going drinking in pubs frequented by leading members of the UFF. She was again questioned about the bag found in her garden and the ground close by. She still refused to answer any questions put to her.'

Jackie was now gaining confidence in her ability to withstand the questioning. 'I think the lads knew me better and that I wouldn't say a word,' she muses. 'There is always an element of paranoia in these circles, but I was confident that no one would think I would squeal about anything because I actually didn't know the nitty-gritty details of any of the events. Johnny always said he trusted me with his life.

'They kept trying to get me to eat, but I didn't eat a morsel the entire time. However, it didn't stop them carrying on the interrogations up until midnight every single day. It got worse with every day. I knew by this stage that they weren't just toying with me, that they had in fact found guns in my back garden and I honestly thought I was going to go down. I tried to figure out how they came to be there. How had I not noticed them? How long were they there? John's finger prints were on them. Because they were on my property I was going to be charged. They brought a gun in and showed it to me. "Have you seen this before?" I genuinely hadn't. I didn't know what this guy had been up to. I was trying to think of anyone who had been out my back. I think they thought this information was going to turn me on the third day, that I would somehow start blabbing a load of stuff. They asked, "Do you know John has been charged with possession of that gun?" I broke down at that point and sobbed.'

Day three was more hectic for Jackie, as by now she knew that most of the top layer of the UFF had also been lifted and it scared her that she was considered on a par with them. Johnny had been there since day two. He ambled through the main corridor shouting out as loud as he could: "Ho, hey, fuck the IRA, and put me in a cell with Jackie Legs!" He found the whole experience nothing more than a comical episode. He used his time to fool around with the police, teasing them with terror tittle-tattle and hinting at 'operations' that lay ahead. "Sure you're on our side, lads!" he'd goad one of the main interrogators. He even reminded them that some of their fellow officers were providing useful intelligence to the UFF terror machine. "Your lot are good for giving us information about those IRA scum. Aren't we doing a good job all the same, given that you can't keep our neighbourhoods safe for us?"

'When I heard him roaring my name out, I thought, you stupid bastard, as I had spent days denying that I knew him,' Jackie says. 'He was screaming his head off and laughing out loud like a hare-brained nutter all the time. It kind of gave me a deeper insight into how ridiculous he was, even in a severe situation. He kept shouting, "Don't let them get to you, Jackie! Stay strong, love." There were quite a number from the Shankill lifted at that time. The police had done a huge round-up. Winkie Dodds got lifted, Fat Jackie Thompson, Coke from the estate, Mo Courtney, all the top loyalists in fact. They had obviously been planning this for at least a few weeks. Castlereagh was filling up. Their line of attack changed with me after Johnny roared out my name. "So you don't know Johnny Adair then, Jackie? And he's screaming

Jackie, aged 28, married and living in Birmingham. Ironically, her nickname in the factory where she worked for seven years before she met Johnny was 'Mad Dog Jackie'.

Jackie, aged 30, after her return to Belfast in 1991. She underwent a huge change of image and began a new life.

Castlereagh Holding Centre, where Jackie was held for interrogation in October 1993. (*Kelvin Boyes*)

The loyalist heartland of Ulster, the Shankill. Pictured here is a little boy talking to a British soldier. (*Kelvin Boyes*)

Gina Adair, brandishing a Union Jack on the walls of Crumlin Road Jail, in protest at her partner's incarceration in 1995. (*Kelvin Boyes*)

Jackie and Johnny at Jackie's house in the Shankill estate, Christmas 1999, seven years into their affair.

Jean (Jackie's mother) and Jackie at the latter's house in Boundary Way. It was nicknamed 'Dallas' by Johnny because of its extravagant décor.

A fashion-conscious Johnny poses for the camera after being sentenced for 'directing terrorism' in 1994.

Jackie's sister Kim died tragically in 2005. Here they are pictured together sharing happier times, New Year's Eve 1999, at the Avenue One Bar, Jim Gray's renowned drinking den.

Jackie Thompson and Johnny Adair—erstwhile pals—capering around the prison yard.

'Simply the Best': Johnny standing proud in front of a prison mural.

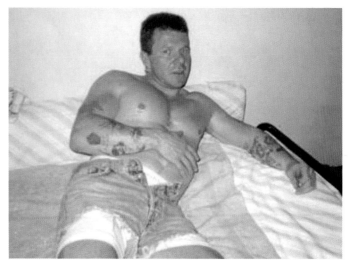

Johnny relaxing in his cell.

'Toy Soldiers': a home-made AK-47, courtesy of the UDA's arts and crafts wing in the H-Blocks.

Prison corridors as well as cells were sumptuously decorated with loyalist murals and red, white and blue bunting.

'Jailhouse Rock': the UDA's very own in-house band of brothers at the Maze Prison.

Prisoners celebrate 12 July 1996 by marching in the prison yard.

The Last Remembrance Sunday, 1999. Adair lays a wreath in the Lower Shankill as the final battle commences for control of the UDA, months before he betrays his comrades.

FRONT, LEFT TO RIGHT: Johnny Adair, Winky Dodds, Mo Courtney and Stephen 'Top Gun' McKeag, all friends together before the fatal fall-out. A year and a half later, Stevie is dead, Dodds is ostracised and Adair is back inside.

Mo Courtney shares a Judas joke with Johnny. Three months later the joke is on Adair as Courtney betrays Mad Dog.

John White, then media spokesperson for the UDA, speaking outside Maghaberry Prison on Johnny's release. (*Kelvin Boyes*)

Johnny and Gina outside their Boundary Way home in 2002, celebrating Johnny's release from jail—although it was to be short-lived. (*Kelvin Boyes*)

Jackie breaks the story of her eight-year affair to a national tabloid in 2003. (*Kelvin Boyes*)

Johnny thwarted on the road to Stormont: John White had plans for Adair to stand for the Northern Ireland Assembly, before things fell apart.

'Sad Dog' (2004), a mural depiction of Johnny's eventual fall from grace, on the walls of the Shankill estate.

your name, Jackie." I didn't answer. I should have said he's probably referring to Jackie Thompson. Maybe he wants to use this opportunity to explore his gay side a bit more.

'The mind games continued unremittingly. When I was being interviewed, they would have Johnny in an adjoining cell so he could hear me getting a bad time. When it was his turn, all I could hear was him laughing and roaring. He was winding them up goodo. Apparently he was telling them he had £180,000 in the bank to buy guns, but if any of them needed a loan he might oblige them. They would come straight back into me then, "Do you know he's got £180,000 in the bank?" I'd look flabbergasted for a second and say: "For God's sake get in there in that case and tell him to buy me a few dresses!" And away they went. When they came back to my cell they said. "No, he said he prefers you with no clothes on." And it went on and on like that; it was almost comical. They were rambling up and down between the cells and feeding back the information to myself and Johnny. But for the fact that it was incredibly abusive, I would have thought I was just dreaming it. At night time though, alone and scared, I thought of my kids and snivelled into the pillow. They kept saying horrendous stuff to me: that I was an ugly slut; that Johnny was only using me because I was a loose slapper; and that my fanny must be as wide as an open umbrella.

'They told me that on the day of his birthday, when he was on his way up to my house, the police stopped two cars in their convoy. Johnny was in one of the cars with some mates, and the other car had other loyalist guys. The men in the second car, when asked where they were going, apparently said, "Up to Adair's girl's house cos she's sure for a good fuck." I got a bit upset when I heard that, but they were only playing a game. They tried to push any button they could find. As time goes on in there the truth gets meshed with lies. It really does. Afterwards I told Johnny about it, and he even looked into it, but obviously it was a lie. They were desperate to get him off the streets by this stage because he was wreaking havoc for the IRA and the police were afraid that the whole thing would end up in a type of civil war. They were getting increasingly frustrated and aggressive when I wasn't giving them a thing. Johnny never did mouth off to me; he never had to. I always knew when something was going down and I had made it a policy not to get involved in that side of things.

'They were coming down heavy on me because they knew from surveillance that Johnny was always with me most of the time, especially at weekends. Even during the week he would say to Gina that he was going jogging and he'd turn up at my house. At the start of the relationship he would only pop in and I wouldn't hear from him for a few weeks, but after a while he got more and more involved with me and was always at my house. That is why I think they regarded me as a soft touch in Castlereagh, that if they insulted me or tested my integrity, I'd break. But I didn't.

'When the solicitor arrived I felt much better, but he did say, "Jackie, you look a bit rough. Are you OK?" A few short days without any food or sleep and I looked like a different person, all ghoulish white and my nerves gone. The solicitor told me my rights, that I was not obliged to tell them anything. I had been told by a friend beforehand to focus on a spot on the wall and that it would help me blank out their conversation. And this is what I did. By day four they were just sitting there falling asleep; they wouldn't even talk to me, at least in the morning time. They knew they would get nothing out of me, especially the one stinking of booze. He had given up the fight, it seems. He was the only one who kept giving me a terrible time. In an afternoon interview he stormed into the room and came right up to my face and said, "You've got blood on your hands." I didn't know what he was talking about. The Greysteel killings had happened the night before, but there was no television or radio in my cell, so I hadn't a clue. He told me about the shootings and asked me was I proud of myself. I told him to fuck off. I had a real bad cough and had asked for a doctor to give me something for it, but they refused. I told them also that I suffered from asthma. It was keeping me awake all night. I still hadn't eaten but I didn't feel weak. My nerves kept me in overdrive. They were begging me to eat; if I collapsed it would be on their heads.'

Q. We want you to tell us about your involvement in the bag containing terrorist articles found in your back garden.

A. Remained silent.

Q. Is there any reason now why you are not talking to us in relation to this matter?

A. Remained silent.

Q. The situation isn't going to change in relation to the interviews. We will continue to ask you questions.

A. Remained silent.

Q. Johnny Adair was arrested last night and requested to be put in a cell next to you, yet you say you don't have anything to do with him. Do you wish to make any comment?

A. Remained silent.

Q. It is obvious to us by the attitude you have adopted in here that you are a dedicated terrorist. Do you wish to deny this allegation?

A. Remained silent.

Q. Your house is being used by terrorists and a large number of men have held meetings there and have been seen leaving your house.

A. Remained silent.

Q. Sunday a week ago, if the IRA had called at your house, just think how many personalities of the UFF/UDA attending a meeting in your house would have been killed, apart from members of your own family.

A. Remained silent.

Q. You are putting the paramilitaries before the safety and well-being of your young family.

A. Remained silent.

Q. You are being used by the UDA, Johnny Adair and his cohorts. Do you not realise that? Are you afraid of what they would do to you and your family if you tell the police the truth?

A. Remained silent.

Q. You are being controlled by the UFF and have been told not to talk to us. You allow them to have meetings in your house and store stuff for them. Can you not see that?

A. Remained silent.
Q. Consider your family, just for once. You owe them that consideration.
A. No reply.

'Subject refused to answer any questions in relation to the finding of terrorist-type articles in her back garden and two shotguns nearby. Tried to encourage her to sever her links with paramilitaries but she refused to be drawn into conversation.'

—

The detectives then tried a different line of inquiry in order to break Jackie down. 'Their new line of reasoning, if you could call it that, was to revert back to aggressive sexual innuendo all the time,' explains Jackie. 'They referred to things like Johnny Adair's reputation as a stallion up the Shankill. One policeman said, "Aye, I heard that all right. It's been all around Belfast." I just sat dispassionately and stared. This went on and on until I snapped. I bent over and said to the female officer. "You should try him out, love. He's unbelievably brilliant in the sack, like he really gives it to you very hard, you know, like you're a bit sore afterwards down there, but it's definitely worth it." She jumped up and howled, "You cheeky fucking bitch!" That's when I knew I had them. That's when I started to really play their filthy game. Two of them got to me more than any of the others, who were just playing the sickly helpers desperate to liberate me from this horrendous relationship with the big murderer Johnny Adair. One of the women irritated me more because she was so attractive you wouldn't think she'd be in that kind of job. She was very good at being aggressive with it. She had blonde hair, a beautiful figure and wore magnificent clothes. She looked like a catwalk model. I took notice of what she wore every day. I wanted to ask her, what are you doing in a job like this? but I didn't, because the minute you get into a real conversation with them, they think they have you. She'd say to me, "Why don't you do yourself a favour and get yourself out of here? He's not worth it. He doesn't give a shit about you, the prick. He'll leave here and pick up someone else to fuck before you even get to the jail. He'll get on with life screwing other women and staying with Gina and his kids."

'I hadn't taken my pill for four days and lay on the bed with bad pains. One female officer just stood there in the cell looking at me. I tried to whisper to her that I had my periods. I was very embarrassed because it was mostly men in there. I asked her if there was any chance she could get me something. She thought when I was calling her over that I was eventually breaking. But instead, she opened the door and shouted all over the corridor. "Oi, you, is there anyone out there? This woman has her bloody periods. Has anyone got a spare sanitary towel or a really big tampon that would fit the likes of her?" It was totally humiliating. I sat and cried when she shut the door. I thought, you complete bastard, just because you lot can't get anything out of me. It was total war after that.'

Q. Would you like to tell us now the truth about what you know about these items found in your back garden?

A. Everything I have told you to date has been the truth. I know nothing about what was found in my back garden.

Q. What about the shotguns?

A. I know nothing about the shotguns.

Q. What day were you last out your back garden?

A. Getting coal the night before.

Q. Do you own a spade?

A. The old man next door lent one to me a couple of times.

Q. Recently?

A. A few weeks ago there was someone in doing the garden.

Q. Did you return the spade?

A. As far as I know it was still there in my garden.

Q. The waste/common ground, have you ever been on it?

A. No, I only ever go to the coal bunker.

Q. The shotguns were found buried in shallow earth in this area. Were you ever in this area?

A. I don't even go up the garden. I've never been in the area you are talking about.

Q. Could these guns ever have been in your home?

A. Never in my home. I have no knowledge of that whatsoever.

Q. Have you been asked or told to keep guns?

A. Never been asked or told to do that.

Q. How long have you lived in your house?

A. Just over a year.

Q. How long have you been socialising in Taughmonagh?

A. More or less since I moved over from the UK.

Q. Do you know Johnny Adair?

A. No comment.

Q. The others we named to you yesterday, Huddleston, Adair, Joe Moore, Green, 'Bubbles' Walsh, Drumgoole, Kerr. Do you know these men?

A. No comment.

Q. Terrorists only leave their weapons with people they can trust. We believe that they trust you and know your house is safe.

A. No comment.

Q. Why did you choose Taughmonagh to live?

A. My husband's family came from there.

Q. Do they still live there?

A. Yes.

Q. Are you connected to the UFF?

A. I certainly am not.

Q. Do you agree with what they do?

A. Don't agree with a lot of things.

Q. Do you agree with the killings?

A. Don't agree with a lot of things.

Q. Would you support the UFF or what they do?

A. No.

'We put it to her that Johnny Adair and these other men mentioned had used her and her home to meet and plan their evil missions and as a result she now found herself in an unenviable position.'

Q. Tell us the truth about these men.

A. No reply.

Q. I'll ask you again. Did these men mentioned earlier visit your house?

A. I can't comment on that.

Q. How often did these people come to your house?

A. They just came and left as people do.

Q. What did they do when they visited your house?

A. Nothing out of the ordinary.

Q. Would you normally sit with them?

A. Just sit in the one room.

Q. Did you make them tea or drinks?

A. The kids make them tea if they need it.

Q. Did you ever hear them discuss anything?

A. I've never heard or seen anything out of the ordinary.

Q. Have you any idea what they talked about?

A. Never seen or heard anything.

Q. Did they ask you to leave them alone at any time?

A. They don't have meetings.

Q. Did they talk about terrorist things?

A. I don't know what they talked about.

Q. Are you afraid of what they might do to you?

A. No reply.

Q. Do these people have a strong hold on you?

A. No reply.

Q. What makes you so frightened of them?

A. No reply.

Q. Have they threatened you in any way or told you to say nothing?

A. No reply.

Q. You are safe from these people. Please tell us about them.

A. No reply.

Q. We believe you know more than what you are saying. Is it that you are afraid or are you trying to protect them?

A. No reply.

Q. We believe these people who came to your home only came for one reason and that was not to socialise or visit you.

A. No reply.

Q. Again, do you consider yourself to be in the UFF?

A. I am not in the UFF.

Q. These people use other people all the time in order to commit acts of terrorism. Are you being used by them?

A. No reply.

Q. The people that come to your house are nothing more than terrorists. Do you accept this?

A. No reply.

'It was quite obvious from the interviews that she has all the characteristics of a hardened terrorist—from refusing to answer any questions to making frivolous complaints on the advice of her solicitor to waste time and mess the police about. It was put to her that she would be continued to be interviewed about her connection to the UFF and about the bag of guns at her house until she left Castlereagh. No matter what we said to her, she still refused to answer any questions at all. She was told that innocent people do not act in this manner.'

Q. Who or how do you put out your wheelie bin?

A. The man next door takes it out for me.

Q. Does anyone hold a grudge against you?

A. I wouldn't know about that at all, would I?

Q. Are you sure there is only one key to your home?

A. Yes.

Q. Have you ever lent your key to anyone?

A. Not to my knowledge.

Q. Did you fit the lock on the front door?

A. Yes, I fitted it myself.

Q. Do you know a road called Southport Court?

A. Never heard of it.

Q. Do you know the Crumlin Road?

A. Not very well. I don't know that side of town at all.

Q. Have you been in that area recently?

A. Haven't been there at all.

Q. When was the last time you were there?

A. About a year ago. I had an accident at Carlisle Circus.

Q. Have you anything further to tell us?

A. No. Everything I have told you so far is the truth.

Q. We believe you allowed terrorists to use your home to hold their meetings in.

A. No. No one has ever used my house. I would not have allowed that.

Q. Why won't you admit to allowing these men use your home and sever your association with them?

A. I've never allowed anyone to use my home.

Q. We believe you had full knowledge of the holdall found in your back garden.

A. I had no knowledge of it whatsoever.

Q. Don't you think you should consider your own family and sever your links with these terrorists?

A. I'm not involved with terrorists; I can assure you of that.

Q. Have you been told not to tell us anything?

A. I've nothing more to tell you.

Day five was more or less the same, interrogations all day long peppered with a few cups of tea and some solitary time in her cell. Jackie was entitled to follow-up visits from her solicitor, but at a certain point in time declined them, preferring instead to chug on alone.

'What was the point when the police would just stand there and listen to your conversation anyway?' she asks. 'The legal firm I was with sent out a second guy who was a bit of a dope, to be honest, but by that time all I wanted was a bit of friendly conversation. I asked for him not to be sent back. I didn't find it that useful. So it was a case of getting through the rest of the interrogations and they came thick and fast like labour pains, the same information over and over and the same replies that I didn't know about the bag and I didn't know what kind of future horror Johnny Adair had in store for the nationalist community etc. The police were losing energy for the mental play-offs as well.

On the third day they had a 'special surprise', as they called it, for me, that the 72 hours were officially up and I was to be kept for a further 48. That was the toughest bit, but the entire experience was nearing an end. One cop really enjoyed giving me that surprise. He stood back like an eejit waiting for me to fall to pieces, but I just said, "Thanks very much" and asked to be sent back to my cell. I heard him scream when I left the interview room, so I guess his surprise backfired and he was the one becoming increasingly frustrated. He really was an awful wanker.

'On day five, I was once again brought breakfast, but yet again I refused it. They brought me toast and a boiled egg. "Just eat a bit of toast". It was tempting as I was feeling very weak; my legs were rattling all by themselves and I was totally exhausted from lack of sleep into the bargain worrying about my kids. In truth I was a wreck by this stage. They took me up for an interview early in the morning and I saw from the corner of my eye Johnny going back to his cell. They had deliberately done that, let our paths cross. He shouted down to me but I never let on I knew him. "Jackie, love, are you all right?" I didn't look around, acknowledge him or anything; I just walked back to my cell. That was hard, but I had to show them that even after five days in a state of vulnerability I was able to hold myself together. The last day was the most nerve-wrecking. I really didn't know what they were going to pin on me, and they had me totally believing I was going to jail.

'At 8 a.m. the doctor paid me a visit. I should have realised when he came in that I would be OK, but my mental health had moved out and gone to live elsewhere. He asked me if I was OK. I said, "yeah, I think so." He asked me if I was capable of going through further interrogations. I said, "Yeah, those assholes may as well get their money's worth out of me." They really badgered me on this final day. "Come on, we know certain murders they've done. You've also got blood on your hands." I said, "Look, at this stage charge me or let me go. You've got fuck all on me." But they kept interviewing me all day long. It was really stressful.'

Strange, but the official interview transcripts, obtained through her solicitor in January 2006, do not reflect this. Even though others have since corroborated that Jackie got a bad time from the officers and endured reams of personal insults, the notes do not reflect this. There is not one expletive in these notes and Adair himself would later support the claim that they called her plenty of names. He later recounted what he heard from his cell. 'They were calling her a dirty English bastard and a whore,' Adair said. 'I heard her squealing back at them. I never expected a woman not to break like that. I heard the police women saying to her, "You're nothing but an ugly bastard", and all sorts of stuff. She stayed totally loyal to me and I didn't expect that. That's when I knew she truly loved me.'

The notes on the final day summarised what had already been said over and over. 'Subject denied all knowledge of the presence of a holdall in her back garden or the shotguns found near by. She stated that she had nothing to do with the Kennedy Way murders and did not support the UFF. We questioned her further about the personalities who frequented her house and held meetings on behalf of the UFF. Subject replied once again that there had never been any meetings at her house. Detective Chief Inspector Graham entered the room at 7.50 p.m. and continued to question her about her involvement with these people. We pointed out as strongly as we could the evils of terrorism and the misery and heartache it had caused so many families on both sides of the community. Subject was then escorted back to her cell by uniformed personnel.'

Despite refusing to co-operate and now on the verge of freedom, her interrogators continued to jibe her. 'At about 8 p.m. they opened the cell door and took me upstairs,' says Jackie. 'All the detectives were standing on the stairwell singing that John Leyton song, "Johnny Remember Me". They taunted me with the lyric and laughed out loud. "Yes I'll always remember till the day I die, I'll hear her cry, Johnny, remember me." I felt I was going down and that they were being deliberately snide. I tried with every last ounce of energy not to react. On the last interrogation, 'X' was sitting there and an older lady. She said to me, "Look, love, it's as simple as this. You're going to be charged", and the main cop said, "You'll be in Maghaberry Jail in the morning, Jackie, but not to worry, I'll get a visiting order and come and see you. You'd like that, wouldn't you, Jackie?" My heart was truly sinking. "I'd love to see you there," I told him. I actually thought he was telling the truth, that he would come and taunt me at the prison if I went down.

'I was utterly petrified. What the frig, I thought, they've got nothing on me. I haven't done anything.' I knew they'd have to come up with something solid but couldn't even guess what it might be. Would it be the guns out the back garden that they were originally going to charge John Crockard with? Were they going to pin it on me instead in order to put pressure on Johnny? That was the end of that boy's relationship with my daughter. I never liked him. He used to disappear and then return back and head straight for the radio; that's a sure sign that he was involved actively. I had warned him off a few times. "Whatever you're doing, do not involve my daughter. Tell her nothing," I had warned him. So many people were involved at that time. I don't think people understand nowadays, but there was a genuine war going on.

'Some time after 8.30 p.m., this huge superintendent came in and looked at me. "Look, Jackie," he said, "all we want you to do is help us put Johnny Adair away." I glared at him and said, "I know fuck all; I don't even know who he is." The other cop said, "You're fucking lying; we know you're lying." The female officer asked, "Would you not, if you found things out, give us a wee ring? We could let on we're working for a charity shop and would bring you down clothes to your house." They must have thought I was completely stupid—bringing charity shop clothes to people's houses and pretending they were collecting stuff to get information at the doorstep—imagine. "Are you charging me or what?" I simply asked. They opened the door and said, "Right, down here." As I walked out, I waited for their final ploy. There were six officers standing around the stairway. I began to walk down the stairs slowly, thinking I was going to jail and I wouldn't see my kids again. My life was totally finished. When I got to the end of the stairs, one of the plain clothes officers said, "Turn back again, back up the stairs." They opened the door at the top, and it was the doctor's room. I walked in, they closed the door behind me and I sat down and burst into tears. The doctor said, "Were you not told you are being released?" When I heard that, I broke down completely, saying over and over, "No, no I didn't, no, no." I was just delirious. He said to me, "You've had a very hard time in here; I don't know how you've done it." I was covered in bruises. I had knocked myself off walls playing the game, pretending they had done it. I had lost it during the interrogations.

'I walked out of his office down the stairs and into the exit office to collect my stuff. They had already rung my daughter at this stage, but I didn't know that. I went back into the cell and got dressed. I was wearing leggings and a loose top. I looked like a tramp. They had kept all my original clothes for forensic purposes. A female officer led me down. I heard Johnny Adair in his cell and I shouted. "Johnny, I'll see you tomorrow, love. I love you!" The police woman turned around and said, "Do you know him?" I replied, "No." She sort of smirked and let go of my shoulder. Get to the gate, get to the gate, get to the gate was all I could think of. There was a petrol station across the road and I would meet my daughter there. My heart was pounding and all I was concentrating on was getting across the road, getting to her and giving her the biggest hug I could. I had convinced myself that they were going to rearrest me at the gate. Was this just another sick game? The key went in the gate, turned and I ran like fuck. I stood across the road for a good ten minutes until a taxi pulled up. My head was reeling. The buzz of the interrogations was still playing through my head like a broken record. My daughter jumped out of the taxi and I just collapsed into her arms. She had to pick me up off the road. The two of us sobbed like babies. "I am so sorry, love. I am so very sorry. I didn't mean to put you through this." But all she could do was cry. I went to my sister Kim's house immediately. My ex-mother-in-law was there and she threw her arms around me. I went into the house and they ran a bath for me. I was so weak I had to be hauled into it. My sister said, "We are going for a drink. We're getting you a brandy." I was weak, really very sick.'

Terror suspects usually go through a second round of interrogation once they are freed without charge from Castlereagh. They are thoroughly debriefed by their organisation's internal security unit, who check to see if their comrade has betrayed any secrets or hatched any clandestine deals with the Special Branch. There was no such debriefing for Jackie. Instead she was met with an unexpected hero's welcome at a UDA drinking den in south Belfast.

'We went straight to the Taughmonagh Club. I walked in and everyone turned and stared at me in total silence. Then they clapped, some ran over and shook my hand, handing me money, buying me drinks. "Jesus Christ, Jackie, not many men get through that, never mind women," they said. The commander on the estate and a few of the other boys from the Ormeau Road congratulated me. I hadn't realised it, but they had got feedback from the solicitor and from others who had been let out earlier. I sat and sobbed when I went home that night. I couldn't let go of my kids. I couldn't get close enough to them. My son always took things in his stride; I felt he was very protected. But my daughter seemed to know more and was visibly affected. I felt so guilty that I had done this to them.'

—

The European Committee for the Prevention of Torture and Inhuman or Degrading Treatment or Punishment (CPT), after visiting Castlereagh in the mid-1990s, concluded in its report: 'Even in the absence of overt acts of ill-treatment, there is no doubt that a stay in a holding centre may be—and is perhaps designed to be—a most disagreeable experience. The material conditions of detention are poor (especially at Castlereagh) and important qualifications are, or at least can be, placed upon certain fundamental rights of persons detained by the police (in particular, the possibilities for contact with the outside world are severely limited throughout the whole period of detention and various restrictions can be placed on the right of access to a lawyer). To this must be added the intensive and potentially prolonged character of the interrogation process. The cumulative effect of these factors is to place persons detained at the holding centres under a considerable degree of psychological pressure.

The CPT must state, in this connection, that to impose upon a detainee such a degree of pressure as to break his will would amount, in its opinion, to inhuman treatment.'

In December 1999, Castlereagh Holding Centre, notorious for the physical and psychological ill-treatment of political suspects, was closed permanently. The centre had been riddled with controversy over claims of police ill-treatment, and its closure was one of the recommendations of the Patten Commission into policing in Northern Ireland. Allegations which led to Castlereagh's reputation for ill-treatment first surfaced in the 1970s at a time when republican violence was at its peak. West Belfast Sinn Féin Assembly member Alex Maskey, who was briefly held at Castlereagh in the early 1980s, told the *Examiner* newspaper when the centre closed: 'There can be no place in the modern world for institutions like it. Many still live with the nightmare of Castlereagh. The brutal litany of physical and psychological abuse meted out by RUC interrogators earned it international notoriety.' However, Maskey, his fellow republicans and their enemies on the loyalist side weren't so up front in their criticism of the terrorists' own form of interrogation that included hours, sometimes days of systematic torture, beatings, sleep deprivation and in the vast majority of cases summary execution without judge or jury.

—

Whilst Jackie was spared an official UDA debriefing, she was still questioned one-on-one by the man she had stayed loyal to in those long hours of interrogation inside Castlereagh. 'Johnny didn't get out until the night after that,' says Jackie. 'At 6 p.m. on the following Monday night he rang and he kept saying, "Jesus, are you all right? I'll be over ASAP. . . . I heard them giving you a terrible time." He came over within an hour. He ran up the driveway, hugged me and said, "Well done." He sat on the chair and looked visibly worried. "Jackie, what did they tell you? Does it change your attitude towards me?" I told him the truth and then I had to face an even harder truth myself. "No, Johnny, it doesn't change a thing. Nothing has changed between you and me, and it never will. If anything, I love you even more."'

04 YABBA DABBA DOO

The night that Gina Crossan burned a tricolour outside Crumlin Road Jail, she turned to the cameras and bellowed, 'Please free my baby', jumped in her car and jetted off to meet with her secret lover, Fuzzy Cousins. That's how devoted Adair's other half was when he was jailed for directing terrorism.

By early 1994 Jackie knew it was only a matter of time before Johnny Adair was towed from the streets for good as sagging peace plans did the rounds. The serving Taoiseach, Albert Reynolds, called for 'demilitarisation' in Northern Ireland, and the Downing Street Declaration of the previous month made possible, room for Sinn Féin to take part in imminent peace proposals if the IRA avowed an undeniable ceasefire. But the reality was that the armed struggle on both sides was heating up to earth-shattering proportions. On New Year's Day, the IRA planted 11 bombs in retail stores and civic buildings in and around Belfast, a move that prompted the UFF to declare that they would continue to respond militarily with brutal force. The next day it fired several rounds at the house of Sinn Féin councillor Alex Maskey's house, and two days after that dispatched two parcel bombs to *An Phoblacht* (Republican News) offices in Dublin.

The organisation had also got its hands on a lethal payload of weapons supposedly sourced from a Lebanese arms dealer, including RPG-7 rocket launchers that were liberally used at the beginning of the second week at the Rock Bar on the Falls Road. Remarkably only three people were injured. The rocket attacks continued recurrently. (Ironically, the weapons originally belonged to the PLO but were captured by Maronite Christians after the Israelis chased Yasser Arafat's organisation out of Lebanon. They were sold to loyalists in 1988.)

On 12 February the UFF carried out a rocket attack on the headquarters of Sinn Féin in west Belfast and again at its offices on the Falls Road on 29 March. Nevertheless, it was the IRA who claimed the first 'successful' fatalities using identical weapons on 17 February, when it killed William Beacom, an RUC officer (two more were injured) during an attack on a police Land Rover in the Markets area of Belfast. Adair's fundamental policy was to "go for the instigators" and the "mouthpieces", as he called them, within the republican movement to achieve maximum impact and undermine the IRA's existence within ordinary nationalist communities.

'I knew Johnny was going to get lifted as the security forces were coming down heavy on everyone for weeks. The situation in the North was deteriorating by the day it seemed,' remembers Jackie. 'There seemed to be prolonged surveillance going on, stake-outs were constant, and the police had given up being discreet about it. I was being watched like a hawk. It was terrible what was going on. While it had been consistently bad in the previous two years, 1994 was truly hellish. It's unbelievable looking back on that time now. It's as if people living in the North didn't have time to comprehend how serious it was. Instead, you found yourself in a state of alert all the time.'

Haphazard sectarian slayings continued on both sides. On 27 January the UFF shot dead John Desmond (51) at his home in the Ormeau Road; a week later, Mark Sweeney (31), another Catholic civilian, was shot dead in Newtownards, Co. Down; Teresa Clinton (34) was shot dead at her home on 14 April, 12 days later; Joseph McCloskey (52) was shot dead at his home in republican New Lodge; just three days later, Paul Thompson (25), a Catholic, was shot and killed while he sat in a taxi in Ballymurphy, Belfast;

and barely two weeks after that, Martin Bradley (23) was murdered in Ardoyne. The UVF were also killing incessantly, claiming 11 deaths by the end of May (including a Protestant woman by mistake, Margaret Wright (31), who was viciously beaten by a group of men and shot four times in the head).

The IRA was also industriously causing widespread devastation with rocket, mortar and bomb attacks across Northern Ireland and in the UK, principally in London. In January, Gerry Adams, then President of Sinn Féin, claimed in a newspaper interview that the 'republican struggle' could go on for another 25 years unless a sustained strategy of peace was put in place. Yet the fledgling peace process was worth preserving for the British, and no one, least of all Johnny Adair, was going to strangle it at birth.

'I had been at a party on Sunday, 15 May, the night before Johnny was arrested, and I left to go to the Shankill with some friends,' explains Jackie. 'We noticed a police car behind us. As we entered a house on the corner of Conway Street, a policeman came right up behind us and followed us into the house, telling us not to move. Two officers asked me to step outside, but I refused, so they called for back-up. Two more constables arrived, lifted me up off the chair, carried me to the car and flung me in the back. I was taken to Antrim Road RUC Station.'

The next day, 16 May, Johnny Adair was detained for questioning about offences in relation to directing terrorism. It came as no surprise to many, as for months Sir Hugh Annesley, the RUC Chief Constable, had intended toppling Adair and his militia. He hand-picked a team of Northern Ireland's top security specialists including the head of Special Branch Ronnie Flanagan, Superintendents Brian McArthur and Derek Martindale, Inspectors Tim Gorrod and as it would turn out, most famously, Jonty Brown, who joined the RUC on Bloody Sunday, 30 January 1972, and became closest to Adair. It was to Brown that Adair chiefly offered details of his exploits, believing rather naively that he was his friend. Brown later told a UTV programme devoted to the RUC's handling of the Troubles in the 1990s: 'I would have taken the view that it was my duty to go right into the heart of the

UFF on the Shankill, or any group. I mean it wasn't just the UFF; the UVF were taking life day in day out and the people in Northern Ireland on both sides of the divide were suffering, and there was, it was my understanding, a clear duty to save life at any time.' Tantamount to 'saving life', as Brown put it, was to get Adair out of the picture.

On 20 May 1994, Adair appeared in Belfast Magistrates' Court accused of 'directing the activities' of the UFF. During the hearing he stood in the dock giggling, smiling and winking at his supporters gathered in the cramped public gallery. By his demeanour he was treating the whole hearing as one big joke. His appearance though sparked extensive rioting throughout Protestant areas in Belfast. It was most pronounced in the Lower Shankill where his followers hijacked buses and taxis to seal off the area.

'When they arrested me the night before, I was left standing in the hallway and I could hear an officer whispering,' says Jackie. 'He came out and said I was being charged with drink driving. I was kept for two hours and they continued to goad me about being Johnny Adair's "bit on the side". "How could you be stupid enough to screw a man like him?" one of them said. He enquired if I knew anything about the "wee man", anything that was going on at all, and if I told them, it would be worth my while, that they would drop the charges of drink driving. I told him to fuck off. His response was, "That's OK so. We'll just drop you off in the middle of Ardoyne and shout out the window, 'It's Johnny Adair's girl', and leave you to it. You're bound to get a really good beating." I told them to go ahead, but I was genuinely scared. Given the dismal atmosphere in the North at the time, I have no doubt I would have been battered or killed if they had left me in a Catholic area. People were seething with anger on all sides and looking for revenge for the flurry of killings that were happening. They drove me to the bottom of Conway Court where I left the party. It was 6 o'clock in the morning. A few hours later I got a call to say Johnny had been arrested and taken to the RUC barracks in Portadown but was later escorted to the Antrim Road RUC Station. I cried my eyes out and rang up asking to speak to him, but they said Gina was there and she was his partner; I had no rights. I asked the man to pass on a message to him, that I loved him and he would hear from me soon.'

Adair was remanded at the Crumlin Road Prison (known as 'the Crum') to appear again in court on 3 June. He seemed in triumphant form, according to close associates, and didn't think that the evidence would stand. The basis of the RUC's evidence was taped recordings of Adair's blustering about terrorist activities to officers during previous questionings which had not been conducted under caution. Looking back on it now, Jackie firmly believes that Johnny put himself in jail, despite a sophisticated police operation to sink him. 'I believe there would have been insufficient evidence if he had resisted the temptation to fly his own kite and brag to RUC officers about his exploits. It was down to him crowing to various policemen about his feats. I mean, everyone used to tell him to cool it. I had been with him plenty of times when we were stopped by the police and he'd boast, "Six Sinn Féiners in so many weeks lads, because you've done nothing about it! Would the Fenians have done that? Would the Provos have done that?" He was telling them what he had done. In a way he was the biggest tout going without meaning to be.'

That night in Belfast, C Company met to discuss the probable outcome and it was decided that if Johnny went down for a stretch that 'Top Gun' Stevie McKeag, considered at the time to be Johnny's right-hand man, should step into Adair's bovver boots as UDA leader on the Shankill Road. Adair may have retained nominal control, but the day-to-day operation of the UDA's notorious C Company passed into the hands of McKeag. It hadn't been that long since McKeag had faced charges himself for the murder of Sean Hughes, a 40-year-old businessman gunned down in his hairdressing shop on the Falls Road, but these charges had been dropped due to lack of evidence.

It had been a trying month for the UFF, as another one of Johnny Adair's close Shankill associates was charged with the rocket attacks on the Sinn Féin offices, and with the murder of an assumed loyalist informer. Gary Witty McMaster, 29, from

Boundary Way, was jailed for life but claimed in court that it was Adair who had shot dead the alleged informer, Noel Cardwell, a mentally challenged young man who was said to have the mind of a 12-year-old child.

In the absence of knowing what to do to further support Adair, more erratic rioting broke out in Protestant areas of Belfast that night, with cars and buses hijacked and set on fire, as well as police patrols being attacked. There were also gunshots heard on the streets although there were no subsequent reports of injuries. If Johnny Adair was attempting to feign innocence as a director of terrorism, the showpiece of strength on the streets was confirming the opposite. 'I knew not to go out that night,' recalls Jackie. 'I told my kids to stay in too. I knew it was going to kick off. I didn't go to the court that day as at that time I still had enough respect for Gina and I didn't want to antagonise her, but I was very shocked when I got the phone call to say he wasn't being released.'

A few weeks later the UDA/UFF took another unpleasant hit. Two of its leading members, Joe Bratty (33) and Raymond Elder (32), were shot and killed by the IRA, walking along the Ormeau Road in Belfast. Up until this point there had been eight attempts to kill Bratty; only six months before he had suffered gunshot wounds to his hands and groin. Elder was apparently targeted after the IRA received information that he had taken part in the killing of five Catholics at Sean Graham's bookies, although the charges had been dropped due to lack of evidence. The UFF without delay issued a threat against all nationalists in the area. For nationalists, particularly those living in the Lower Ormeau Road and Markets areas, fear of UFF retribution was mixed with glee that two hate figures of loyalism in south Belfast had been removed from the scene.

The Crum was an especially run-down Victorian prison (it was shut in 1996) and was almost 150 years old by the time Johnny had settled into his cell. According to BBC archives, an underground tunnel links the jail to the courthouse opposite, and it is thought that the term 'going down' was coined when prisoners were taken from the court to the jail. When operational,

it had 640 cells in four wings, and while its first inmates were
forced to walk to its daunting entrance in chains, many of its
modern-day prisoners felt similarly 'chained', with loyalists and
republicans being forced to integrate. On Saturday, 16 July, about
a hundred inmates tore apart their cells and used bricks, chunks
of wood, metal bars from the beds and other materials to break
out on to the roof and spark an unprompted riot. Johnny of
course was one of the agitators, doing a great impression of an
excited Neanderthal waving his arms about on the roof, just in
time for the media's arrival. He was unmistakably seen on several
news bulletins that night gesticulating wildly, roaring "yeheyyy!"
and egging on fellow insurgents. Mad Dog was clearly enjoying
the attention.

'I remember that day vividly,' says Jackie. 'I was feeling quite
down thinking about Johnny and I got a phone call from a friend
who said, "Turn on the news, you'll never guess who's on the roof
of the Crum." I turned the TV on and there was Johnny jumping
up and down like an eejit. I thought it was hilarious.'

The UDA quickly informed the media that there was a protest
taking place outside the prison. This is when Gina was seen
burning a tricolour and screaming for her partner's release.
Another well-known loyalist woman ran at journalists with a
baseball bat, threatening to 'kick the shit' out of them; another
had brought along a CD player to play chart tracks for prisoners
who began dancing on the roof. The protest did actually help the
prisoners' plight and arrangements were made to move a glut of
prisoners to the Maze. The authorities didn't have much choice as
the prison was so abysmally damaged—a minor victory for Adair
and his chums.

'Everyone who was behind bars at the Crum hated the place,'
said Jackie. 'It was old and bleak with virtually no facilities. The
men thought the Maze was a holiday camp by comparison. There
they had snooker tables and a canteen, plenty of recreational
space, their own wings and outdoor yards to march around in.
Each cell was done up like an individual sitting room—they were
free to choose their own wallpaper borders, curtains, duvet covers
etc. The prisoners were happy that they were being held in wings

according to paramilitary affiliation. That was a very important aspect to making them feel safe and secure, and of course it meant they could organise themselves that wee bit more.'

The site of the prison had originally been used when internment was introduced to deal with increasing violence back in 1971. At that time, ministers backed by London decided to use the Special Powers Act in an effort to take those it believed responsible for violence off the streets. However, at the start it was predominantly republican prisoners who were held in elongated huts at the disused air-base known as Long Kesh. In 1976, a more sturdy structure was opened in the form of eight H-blocks with a 17 foot high concrete perimeter wall. Every H-block contained 96 single cells separated into four wings of 24. Twelve 30 foot army watch towers were situated around it. Over the 30 years of the Troubles, there were countless killings, beatings and riots at the Maze, as well as attempted break-outs. The prison itself became very politicised and after the accomplishment of the 1981 republican hunger strikers led by Bobby Sands to demand certain rights as 'prisoners of war', both sides became much more systematic in managing their wings or blocks. Johnny, for example, carried on directing terrorism fruitfully from within the jail, passing on commands to visitors who would take messages to C Company and the wider UFF on the outside. Effectively Adair and his comrades, like their republican opponents, ran the jail's interior.

'There were murals all over the walls on their wings just like there were in the Protestant estates on the outside,' says Jackie. 'Prison officers had to negotiate with the OC [Officer Commanding] of each wing before they could carry out any searches or other jobs. The prison wasn't run by the prison authorities; it was run by the prisoners, plain and simple. Some of the lads used to call it "Camp Maze".' (Wags in Belfast could be forgiven for calling it 'Holiday Camp Maze'.)

Johnny was filmed by a BBC documentary team against a backdrop of wall murals, some of which read: 'Yabba, Yabba, Doo, Any Fenian Will Do' (a sick take on Fred Flintstone's famous dictum) and 'Kill 'Em All, Let God Sort 'Em Out'. The loyalist murals were mainly military-style regalia, uniforms, shields, guns and lots of ghoulish proclamations about battles won. There was also a fair scattering of lurid semi-naked women beautifying recreational areas and keeping the men company. In the mid-1990s, the prison authorities allowed 24 hours' freedom of association in the wings. A lot of prisoners, however, were devoting more and more time to discussing the possibilities of peace and their place in acquiring it. At least some of the paramilitary bosses who led this thinking on both sides inside the H-blocks were instrumental in achieving the ceasefires of 1994, it is believed.

Camp Maze slowly built up a regular stock of smuggled goods, including alcohol, mobile phones, porn and even animals, according to Jackie. Even as far back as 1981 republican prisoners had miniature crystal radio sets smuggled into the jail so they could hear the reaction on the outside to the prolonged strikes. When not in use, they would conceal the radios in their bodies. In Jackie's time of visiting the Maze, it was mainly the women who were the couriers of smuggled goods. The commerce of smuggling would continue to increase throughout the 1990s, as would shortly become clear three years down the line when guns and wire cutters were smuggled into the jail to facilitate the murder of founder and leader of the Loyalist Volunteer Force (LVF), Billy Wright. The means for doing so was not that ingenious. It just took a bit of common sense to realise that visitors were not searched at certain times of the year such as around Christmas time. The penalty for smuggling was banned visits for three months, not a colossal punishment by any means.

'We used to smuggle in vodka in balloons in our knickers; walking about normally they'd just feel like jelly, and if you moved to the rhythm they wouldn't be seen,' says Jackie. 'We would get searched when we went in, but it wasn't particularly thorough at the time. You go into a wee room where two women search you. One takes your bag; the other searches you down, goes through your pockets and sometimes takes one boot or shoe off. But if you were, say, bringing in some cannabis/blo, you'd have to put that in the crack of your arse. Because the Troubles were so high level at the time, I think that prison staff were concerned about repercussions if they upset the visitors of paramilitaries. The male prison officers were so terrified of some of the male prisoners and their visitors that they barely frisked them at all. It was cubicles in the meeting hall area. I was there the day one of the lads smuggled in a parrot. Biggs called me over. "Wait until you see this, Jackie." There was this bird in a sock; they had drugged the wee thing to keep it quiet. Johnny came up with the idea of having a pup smuggled in; other animals followed. One of the fellas put the drugged pup down his trousers in a little sack, but they hadn't given it enough sedatives and it started whimpering and was discovered. He wanted a load of animals— a kind of zoo within a zoo, I suppose.'

It seemed that Adair turned Doctor Doolittle had little to do but spend time with his makeshift Noah's Ark; his republican counterparts, on the other hand, devoted much of their spare time studying for BA degrees and reading political and historical books insatiably. (The prison library is now based in Belfast's Linen Hall Library and stocks a myriad of texts from this time.) Johnny and his indoor troops organised time-consuming meetings on various issues of significance and also kept busy manufacturing wooden guns and other mock-up armoury and a whole stock of loyalist souvenir goods churned out to raise funds for the LPA. Most of their women (wives and girlfriends) on the outside would have been desperately stuck for cash and the LPA helped raise funds for their basic needs. It's also why the notion of prisoner releases played an important part of any would-be peace proposals. A poster used by the LPA in 1994 depicted a blackened face of a man with a military watch tower in the backdrop. It was reproduced from the flag of the National League of POW/MIA families representing American soldiers still presumed to be prisoners of war or missing in action in Vietnam. It bore the simple message, 'Send Our Prisoners Home'.

'A lot of prisoners were exceptionally clever. It wasn't until they were sent to jail that they realised they had astonishing talents,' Jackie maintains. 'It's sad that they had to sink that far before realising they possessed real gifts; they were too busy living life to the full and fighting the cause. I remember being sent amazing stuff from the Maze: music boxes in the form of castles made from lollipop sticks, intricate hankies with loyalist slogans, and wonderful paintings of the royal family and other loyalist themes. Half of these people were artists and didn't know it.' We will never know what positive use such skills could have been put to, but for the war.

An alternative much-loved distraction for Johnny was the setting up of his very own kangaroo court, a kind of haphazard extra-legal judicial assemblage of jailed paramilitary figures judging fellow jailed paramilitary figures. One online dictionary definition of a kangaroo court describes it as 'a court characterised by dishonesty or incompetence' and this best fits what was going on at the Maze in 1994. The system of mock justice was set up purely for jailhouse amusement, although the idea was that new recruits would not know if it was serious or not.

'The men filled their time with practical jokes,' says Jackie. 'They seemed to get more inventive the longer they were in there. I remember Johnny ringing me one time, in stitches laughing. "Wait until I tell ye what we did, Jack," he said. This young fella had come on to the wing, and they showed him his cell and told him he had to keep it clean and ran through a whole host of other internal rules. They told him he had to come to a certain room at a certain time, which he did. He sat on a chair and a couple of them gathered around. Johnny said, "We've got something to tell you. We received word from a very reliable source on the outside that you're a tout." The kid nearly shit himself. Before he could open his mouth, another one of the guys said, "Shut up! The word on the wing is you're a tout and that's the end of it. We want to know what you've been touting about." The kid started to cry a bit. Johnny, of course, tried to console him. "I'll tell you what it is," he said. "I'll give you these tablets, because when those boys get their hands on ye, they're going to beat you up or hang ye, so you may as well take these and they'll help ye not feel it." It was just a bit of fun in their eyes. The panic in the young guy's face was unbelievable, according to Johnny, and he had to really fight to keep a straight face. So the young guy headed off to his cell shaking, with the tablets in his hand. They gave him ten minutes before going after him to tell him it was only a joke. I said to Johnny, "For fuck's sake, he could have done himself in. That's not funny." Your mind is in a state of shock when you go into prison and it's the last thing you need. They were continuously playing jokes like that. They'd put acid in people's drink or food and goad them: "See that bloke over there. He's watching you; someone heard him say this morning at breakfast that he plans on killing you." Everything was fun on the inside. It's a wonder that their antics never backfired harmfully. Don't forget that a person's mind is very paranoid when in prison. There was mistrust and suspicion on the outside throughout the Troubles, but it was ten times worse inside. They cashed in on that paranoia and turned it into a form of entertainment.'

Such entertainment merely reflected the bizarre mix of childishness and menace that permeated the loyalist paramilitary underworld, especially the UDA. The late John McMichael's bodyguards used to think it amusing to superimpose the heads of UDA leaders taken from news photographs on to the svelte and naked bodies of porn models and post them up on the organisation's main notice board when the media called around for interviews. Mock-up trials, a zoo inside the Maze, sex on tap and so on in the Adair era were merely the continuation of a long lineage of childish, lewd behaviour.

Prisoners were, within reason, in control of their own visits. This not only meant who came to the jail but how long they stayed. This was important, given that they were able to exert great pressure on their communities outside. In general, inmates were left alone with wives and girlfriends (and mistresses), with plenty of time to exchange gifts, news, messages, and even sexual acts.

'At the Maze the cubicles were high, and no one looked over each other's booths because it was a given that intimate stuff might be going on,' says Jackie. 'Everyone knew that partners were going to have sex, oral, hand-jobs, the full whack. A lot of women wore no panties and sat on their men's knees and did the business that way without so much as a squeal. These men were ravenous when behind bars; politics wasn't their only hunger that needed feeding. When a man is in prison he needs a tender touch to keep him going. At the Crum it had been different as the visiting area was more open plan, but sexual acts still went on regardless.'

Jackie would later find out just how imperative that 'tender touch' was to Adair when he fought the war from inside his wallpaper-with-borders cell. Jackie maintains that a few of the top men's women got pregnant while their sweethearts were serving long sentences, including a male relation of Johnny's, much to the woman's consternation who didn't need another child when the main source of income was going to be languishing behind bars for two decades. She got pregnant twice while her husband was in for attempted murder. He had chased a man with a hatchet and ran amok with the weapon.

A number of women went into 'service' for Adair's loyalist soldiers—'service' meaning sex on a regular basis with his jailed cadres. 'There was a girl from Tiger's Bay, a well-known prostitute —she worked in a loyalist-run brothel—who began sending in pornographic photographs for Johnny and his crew,' remembers Jackie. 'In them, with her legs spread wide open, she was using a vibrator. These photos were spread all around the prison. Johnny thought it was brilliant. I heard she not only sent him photos but had also visited him in the Maze. When I tackled him about it, he denied it. Then I got a call from a friend to say that the prostitute had been up to see Johnny a few times. Whether it was just a friendly visit or not, who knows?

'Apparently on one visit she just had a Mac on her. On the word of this friend of mine, all she had on under the Mac when she went in to be searched was a bra, knickers, stockings and suspenders. When I asked Johnny about it, he didn't deny it. He said, "Ah sure, she was giving a couple of the lads a wank and stuff, you know. Nothing hectic, Jackie." When I asked if she touched him, he just sniggered and said, "Of course not, Jack." But the girl herself told me a few years later that she did "give Johnny pleasure" inside the jail. She certainly wasn't visiting him to offer spiritual guidance or to talk politics, that's for sure. I mean this was going on when men on the outside were working towards a peace process!'

Incongruously, their loyalty didn't last for long. That same girl was put out of her housing estate during the loyalist feuds of 2000 and viciously beaten for supposedly giving information about John 'Grugg' Gregg's boat journey that he took back to Belfast from Scotland in early 2003 on the night he was killed. It was later discovered that Johnny had aided the running of brothels during his time in prison and during some of his parole breaks, helping the lurid enterprise along by handing out cards to women in loyalist areas to entice them to work for paramilitary-run bordellos. It was also known that prisoners on parole, whose libidos had also undergone a harsh sentence, were given 'free' trips by Johnny to the brothels on release. Clearly the C Company commander cared for the welfare of his troops!

'I send them over to have a good screw, Jackie, that's all. I look after my men. They've served time for me you know,' he once enlightened her. 'I told Johnny that sending a horned-up man over to someone who had been bucked by half of Belfast and was probably full of disease was hardly a good way of looking after a person, but he didn't see my logic at all,' Jackie remarks. 'I knew all about that girl; she wasn't the cleanest, but apparently she was very experienced. She was into all this three-in-a-bed business and more besides. She told me that personally, but I'm still not sure if it's actually true or if she was just bragging. She said she had had sex with Johnny and another high-ranking UDA man at the same time. According to her, she'd had sex with most of the high-up ones. Now some of these men would have had more interest shaking hands with the IRA than using a condom, so I can only imagine what this woman was carrying in her, apart from her stories.'

However, back at the Maze in 1994, what is even more startling is that the prison officers allegedly let this young hustler stroll on up into the visiting area half naked in her flasher's Mac. It seems probable that in the circumstances sex acts were bound to take place. Perhaps they thought it might be useful to pacify some of the more risky or belligerent prisoners, that it may somehow make their working lives more trouble-free. After all, prison officers themselves were often victims of prison politics. One such officer told BBC news exactly how the loyalist prisoners executed their threats. 'Sometimes you would be told directly by the RUC that they had intelligence on you. Sometimes they would talk within earshot of an officer and reveal details about a colleague's life—who his wife was, what car he drove, where he went for a drink—and then you'd know that they were really serious.' Prior to the 1994 ceasefire and the Good Friday Agreement 29 prison officers who had served at the Maze were murdered by paramilitaries and 50 officers took their own lives, presumably from the strain of the job. So it's understandable that while working during the zenith of the Troubles in Northern Ireland, prison staff made allowances that would not have been tolerated in any other prison in the world. The reality of sex, drugs and rock 'n roll being perfectly amalgamated into prison life would be an unfeasible pipedream to the 3,373 prisoners on America's Death Row today, for example.

Meanwhile, as Johnny 'controlled' his visitors and guests, it meant that Gina was given preference in the beginning, being his enduring partner and the mother of his three children. Jackie was relegated to love-locum, at least for the first few months. 'I was up and down to the prison myself anyway visiting a friend, so I would see Johnny on visits sitting there yapping away to Gina. It was hard,' she says. 'I was always aware something wasn't quite right with their visits. They seemed to be constantly engrossed in heated arguments. She always sat there with her head down. It was odd because most of the women were very emotional during visits, hugging and kissing their men. It was hard seeing him like that from across the room, but I got letters from him soon enough and messages were passed on through friends to me. There was talk at the time of them getting married and maybe having another baby, which cut me up a bit I have to say. Under normal circumstances anyone would assume that the "other woman" is just a sideline, but he constantly took the piss out of her and had told me at that stage that he would never marry her. She had already tried to organise a secret wedding some time before and he went ballistic. He bought her a jeep instead as a consolation prize. (He later took that jeep off her when she slept with one of his "trustworthy" men.)

'As the prison officers needed permission to get on to the wings, Johnny and his crew could pretty much do what they wanted. It was a few months in when he managed to get himself a mobile phone. They weren't that widespread at the time and expensive to use. I had just got back from Corfu on a holiday when a friend who was staying at my house said to me, "Someone's going to phone you in a while." It was Johnny. I couldn't believe it! "Where did you get the phone?" I asked him. "Sure you know me, I can get anything I want in here," he said. His bills were astronomical—at least £1,000 to £2,000 a month from ringing myself and Gina and whoever else he was staying in contact with. The UDA paid those bills. I cried when he rang because I knew now that even if I couldn't see my man, I could at least hear his voice as he swore he'd ring every day, which he did.

'There was a lot of drugs and booze smuggled in, especially for prison weddings, of which there were a lot. I even remember Johnny showing me photos of prison officers smoking dope with inmates and stuff, so they were definitely aware of what was going on. It was the middle of the Troubles and a lot of the men who were inside and feeling unsure of their future wanted to get married, I suppose to feel better. When a man goes to prison he becomes very insecure in his relationship. Somehow getting married balanced things out. They really do think they love you when they're in prison; it's when they come out you realise things change.

'I noticed after a few months that Johnny was very nervous and agitated all the time; he couldn't believe he'd been put in prison. Though he acted the Jack the Lad during the day, when he was on the phone to me at night he was a totally different person. Everything was a joke in front of other people, but behind it all he was in bits, really stressed and upset all the time—I would even say depressed. He wasn't coping at all. He used to say to me, "It's all right for you; you're really strong." I used to tell him in return, "Why don't you stop pretending you're a hard man, because you're not." Friends of his also saw a huge change in him. He heard that Gina wasn't playing the devoted "other half" role too well, and that didn't help.'

From the time Johnny was held in remand at the Maze, the war on the outside continued apace. In June it was reported that the IRA was 'considering a ceasefire', although there was little let-up with the killings on either side. Just a week after a newspaper carried the report alluding to a potential end to the hostilities, the UFF shot dead Joseph Donaghy (33) at a Tyrone golf club. Donaghy was yet another Catholic civilian. Two days later the IRA murdered Raymond Smallwoods (44), a high-ranking member of the UDA and a member of the political wing, the Ulster Democratic Party (UDP). This was a huge setback as Smallwoods was very politically oriented and was not averse to the idea of a peace settlement. At least half a dozen more civilians were arbitrarily killed by the UFF before the end of the summer. In September, Taoiseach Albert Reynolds shook hands with Gerry Adams, President of Sinn Féin, and John Hume, then leader of the SDLP, a move that was highly criticised in the media and by senior loyalists who suspected (wrongly as it turned out) that there was a secret deal arranged between the British government and the IRA.

'It was impossible to keep up with everything that was happening politically,' says Jackie. 'You just lost track. Every day I'd listen to the news and there'd be just as many Semtex finds as news clips about this side having successful talks with that side, and what have you. At the same time the killings were still going on and no one knew what was going to happen next. In the estates most of the women's men were locked up or were being dragged in by the police continuously. There was definitely a determined effort to get some kind of peace in place, but most of us knew that the politicians had little chance. You have to remember that by this stage so many families [on both sides] had lost people and wanted revenge, no matter how much they talked of peace. While everyone wanted it "one day", there was still a thirst for vengeance in a lot of working-class areas that had suffered most during the 1980s and early 90s.'

That peace, however, did temporarily arrive. On 1 September, the IRA enacted its unequivocal ceasefire and later, on Thursday, 13 October, a loyalist ceasefire was announced by the Combined Loyalist Military Command (CLMC). 'The permanence of our ceasefire will be completely dependent upon the continued cessation of all nationalist/republican violence', the statement read. The proceedings were led by Gusty Spence, a time-honoured member of the UVF. The CLMC offered 'abject and true remorse' to 'innocent' victims of loyalist violence. Key UFF figures including John White—fast becoming Adair's mentor—stood shoulder to shoulder with Spence at the historic press conference to announce the ceasefire. It had only been passed of course with the prisoners of both loyalist factions agreeing to the cessation. Adair, for now at least, was on message despite staring down the barrel of 15 years in prison.

Albert Reynolds later haughtily announced: 'This decision effectively signifies the end of 25 years of violence, and the closure of a tragic chapter in our history.' It was a rather rash prediction, with the likes of Adair and Co. only lukewarm towards the cessation. The ceasefire, as well as being legitimate, would also open up a new era of 'no claim, no blame', where paramilitaries who 'took out' members of divergent communities would not own up to the killings and thereby jeopardise the ceasefire. While Northern Ireland continued to rock itself into a diplomatic lull, Johnny Adair's love life had begun a new war all of its own. A few months into the sentence, Johnny got word that Gina had at least one fancy man, if not several. Jackie herself thought there was something going on and regularly saw Gina driving around the Shankill wearing make-up and looking dolled up, which was uncharacteristic for a known hardliner UFF woman.

'I got a phone call from a friend of mine to say that Gina was seeing someone. I was really shocked,' says Jackie. 'It was less than six months into Johnny's sentence. I honestly believe she couldn't do without sex, plain and simple, and was prepared to risk anything to get it, including the lives of other men if Johnny found out. Johnny once told me that Gina had a very healthy sexual appetite. He used to say of her quite casually, "Ah Gina loves the dick." He seemed full of pride about her libido even when it was clearly not being directed his way. I knew something was up because Gina had been getting someone to child-mind her kids when she headed off to baby-sit elsewhere. She was actually baby-sitting for Paul and Elaine Orr, and while they went out she had Fuzzy over. This was allegedly around the same time she had been seeing Paul (Paul got a bad beating just after).

'Winkie Dodds and Big Donaldson told her that she had to tell Johnny or she'd be in for a hiding. They were concerned about Johnny freaking out completely if he heard it from inside the jail, so off she went to tell him. They gave her two days. What happened next should have been a sign of what lay ahead for me with regard to their mind games. She got on the phone and told Johnny that Fuzzy had told her all about me (which she knew already) and began screaming about him having an affair with Jackie Legs. He and Gina both played a dangerous game when it came to love. Neither of them was monogamous. I don't believe he was sleeping with other women for the first few years we went together, but even when he was in prison he had different girls going up and down to see him. All the paramilitary men had reams of women desperate to give them attention. He denied point blank that he was seeing me, which I understand in the context. "I'm not seeing that blonde nut!" he told Gina. So by the time she went up to face him, he was already a co-accused. Then he got on the phone to me crying like a baby. I told him to calm down, but he just kept repeating himself, "How could she do this to me when I'm banged up in here?" I wanted to say to him, well, when you're banged up she's not averse to being banged up either, but just in a different way. Instead, I asked him where she was now, and he said she had gone out to clear her head. But she had gone to warn Fuzzy that everything was now out in the open. Fuzzy was a married man at the time and his wife was expecting a baby. I suppose you could say it was a bit of a mess. He kept telling me over and over how he couldn't live without her. Telling me! Like an idiot, I calmed him down and told him what to do. I gave him Fuzzy's number. As I had had a run-in with Fuzzy on the street the week before, when he called me a slut, I had no loyalty towards him. I knew Johnny would ring and intimidate him, but I didn't care. I told Johnny that I would pull away there and then and leave him and Gina to it, but he kept pleading, "No Jackie, I need you, I need you" and I fell for that. On the one hand he was telling me he couldn't be without this woman, and on the other he was telling me he couldn't do without me being around to melt my brain. The fact that I went on after this point means I must have been totally dense. But when you love someone to that extent you'll do anything for them no matter what. Johnny just kept phoning me. The more his private life got into a mess, the more he rang me to know what to do about it even though I was also part of his private life. It was becoming increasingly fucked up.'

Jackie was correct in her assumption. Fuzzy later had his arms broken and when he did eventually ramble back to his wife, he was forced to live behind reinforced doors. Gina fell pregnant during this time and Adair gave her £500 for an abortion. He simply couldn't bear the thought of Gina having a child with another man, even if they were on the verge of a lasting break-up. The ensuing irony here is that Jackie firmly believes that there is at least some level of uncertainty as to the paternity of the couple's last child, as he was conceived during the 'steroid years', when Johnny was pumping his body full of anabolic steroids that are now known to potentially result in temporary sterility. This was also the time when Jackie herself was actively trying for a child with Adair, to no avail, despite attempting for years. It made little sense to her as she had previously fallen pregnant effortlessly with her husband in Birmingham and was always very fertile herself. 'It's only a theory,' maintains Jackie, 'but I always wonder why in six years of trying for a child with Johnny, I didn't get pregnant and it was throughout that time that he'd got into the steroids. Well, they're supposed to shrink your nuts and reduce your sperm count, but we'll never know.'

Johnny and Gina's relationship ruptured, albeit temporarily in late October 1994, ironically during the first phase of loyalist political 'peace', and Jackie was given the green light to take over as the leading starlet in Adair's swashbuckling stage play that was his love life. It seems incredible that his mounting harem of partners, mistresses, groupies and prostitutes would have played such a central role in his life during the most fragile political climate for decades, but it looks as if he was prolifically needy.

The end of 1994 and early 1995 was the most stable period in Northern Ireland's history post-1969. There was a real sense of optimism around summed up by the Van Morrison song 'Days Like This', which would become an anthem for Bill Clinton's historic visit to Belfast in the autumn of 1995. Loyalist and republican prisoners' morale was raised as much as the general populace's outside. The inmates locked up in the H-blocks were told by their external leadership that there would be a post-ceasefire deal which would secure their collective early release from prison. So Adair on the one hand and the IRA leadership in the other H-blocks of the Maze allowed their political allies on the outside to negotiate on their behalf. For a brief, bucolic period in the mid-1990s it seemed Mad Dog and the rest of the C Company killing machine was finally at rest.

When first the IRA ceasefire broke down in February 1996 and then loyalists returned to war under various *noms de guerre* such as the Red Hand Defenders (RHD), Adair was back as he said 'behind the ball again', running the terrorist campaign from inside his cell through mobile phones and a series of coded messages. He and C Company almost helped scupper the 1998 Good Friday Agreement when at the beginning of that year the Lower Shankill unit went on the rampage after Adair's friend Billy 'King Rat' Wright was assassinated inside the Maze. Only for the intervention of Mo Mowlam (who went into the jail to plead with Adair to call off the campaign) and immense political pressure on the UDA on the outside, C Company would have kept on killing, thereby creating the danger of sucking the IRA into renewed conflict and consequently there would have been no peace deal and maybe no ceasefire. Even behind bars Adair was still playing a central role right up to the Good Friday Agreement deal and beyond.

On a personal level it would be another 11 years before Adair eventually split from Gina for good, the end of the affair being a salaciously unromantic occasion. In Old Station Park in Bolton, UK, in October 2005, after his exile from Belfast and just hours after he was released from a 39-day stint in prison on harassment charges, Adair punched, kicked and dragged her along the ground by her hair. He had been told once again when he was in prison that Gina was sleeping with a young exiled loyalist in his early 20s who had previously sworn his allegiance to Adair. It was as much as Johnny could take after being locked up for so many years. He does, after all, expect total loyalty from all his followers, even to this day.

'News travelled fast that Johnny and I were at last a real couple,' reminisces Jackie. 'A lot of people came up to me around the Shankill and shook my hand to congratulate me. The only person that was nasty towards me was Sam "Skelly" McCrory, who sniggered in my face and said, "At last you got what you wanted, Jackie Legs." He was very protective of Johnny, but we all know why. It's no secret that Skelly is gay, and it's my personal opinion that he had fancied Johnny since they were young. I eventually had it out with him, telling him to "go get a fucking boyfriend of your own and leave mine alone." The lads in the UDA had a great laugh about that, although some of them thought it was foolish of me to stand up to him as he could be quite dangerous. He had quite a temper on him.

'At first when I used to visit Johnny at the Maze, and after he had finished with Gina, he seemed happy. She was pleased too to get the freedom she wanted for so long. He was trying to get on with things and it gave us a chance to keep our relationship going. But I also began to see his mind go quite quickly and I became very confused. He didn't want her, but he was phoning her all the time and would then phone me moaning about what she said to him. What he didn't realise was that the authorities were listening in when they used the mobile phones. I think that's why they allowed the mobile phones on the wings. I used to say to him, "Do you not realise they're listening to you?" And he'd laugh and say, "Don't be stupid, Jack, of course they're not." He was either playing dumb or was truly dumb at the time. I'm sure the prison officials must have regarded Gina and Johnny as being completely off their heads, the way they went on and the sick mind games. And then they must have looked at me running up and down to the prison all the time and thought, she's a bloody nut too. I realised too that Gina was goading him about having a small cock when he was in jail. He'd ring me crying, "Jackie, is my dick an OK size? Jackie, am I an ugly bastard?" and I'd reply, "Is that silly cow ringing up insulting you? Tell her to fuck off." He rang me one time asking me should he shave his balls. I thought I was going mad. "Where are you getting this from?" I asked him. "Gina said it's all the rage, it's what all the men are doing now."

'No matter how much I gave to Johnny, he and Gina had a bizarre co-dependency that to this day I do not understand. I always believed, and still do, that she had a very strong hold over him, that she knew something powerful or important about him that he would always bow to her every demand, regardless of how many times she crossed him. Gina herself was very "involved" in the whole scene, but I think whatever she knew about him was even bigger still.'

At the same time as the partner 'switch' was going on, bizarrely Gina asked Johnny if Jackie would baby-sit their three kids. It was an unusual choice of minder but not a wholly incomprehensible one. Perhaps Gina wanted to check out the competition and get to know Jackie a little better. If Gina was serious about Fuzzy, telling her close associates that he was the 'love of her life', Jackie thought that maybe she was ready to take her seriously.

'It was so strange going around to her house for the first time to collect the kids. She was going away with Fuzzy for the weekend. Johnny gave me her phone number and I had rung earlier that morning to arrange it. After being public enemies for so long, it felt truly odd behaving amiably with each other. She used to call me the 'old dog with the good figure' and told everyone at that time that I was 48 years old (I was 35 at the time). She constantly bitched about me and spread rumours that I was into black men. I arranged to pick the kids up on a Friday night. She seemed OK towards me, to be honest. I asked her if she wanted my phone number to check on them, but she said no, that they'd be fine, which really surprised me. I know I would never let a stranger look after my kids or at least not without a contact number. I found out later she had gone to Portrush with Fuzzy and his friends, hunting. This was about the time she started getting into drugs in a big way.

'The kids were really lovely I have to say. They were very mannerly children and exceptionally well behaved. Johnny absolutely adored them and wanted them brought up "properly" as he often told me. And I think in fairness they had done a good job together. I was very warm towards them. I love children anyway; I always have. Chloe was only about 2 years old at the time; she was such a gorgeous little girl. She always wanted to play. She'd run up to me all the time and fling her arms up for a cuddle, chuckling out of her. Natalie was that bit more shy. She'd ask to sleep in with me at night and I'd tell her that her dad sent a kiss for her and I'd try to reassure her that everything was going to be OK. Jonathan was also a lovely child. I think at the time he felt the upheaval with his parents the worst. He asked could he come and live with me a few times. It was hard for him because he was nearly a teenager and it is upsetting for any child to see their parents in turmoil. I knew that more than anyone from my own life.'

It seems Jackie's conjecture wasn't far wrong. Jonathan Adair was charged with selling heroin and crack cocaine to undercover police officers on the streets of Bolton in Lancashire in 2003. Following a dawn raid by UK police at his home, a wad of cash was discovered that could not be accounted for, as well as a crossbow, body armour, a drug dealer's debtor list and fake guns. The year before, Jonathan Adair was shot in both legs at Florence Square in the loyalist Shankill Road. At first it was reported that his father was 'shocked and devastated' at the attack and had no prior knowledge of any attempt to harm his son. However, it later transpired that Adair himself ordered the shooting as a result of his son's anti-social behaviour in the community. It was a sardonic recurrence of Johnny's own teenage life that had forced him into the youth segment of the UDA. 'As a parent I can put my hand on my heart and say that you'd need to be insane to order the shooting of your own child,' asserts Jackie. 'When the truth about that came out in recent years, I felt sick to the stomach and grateful that I didn't have a child with Johnny after all.'

As well as the new 'love of her life', Gina began to see other men and taunted Johnny in jail about who she was going out with. She kept in touch with him unbeknownst to Jackie, and shared details of her sexual encounters with him. Lurid tales of the latest sexual crazes including bondage, burning body parts with candle wax, the latest sex toys and using 'knives' in bed on private parts, were the hot topics of the day. It drove Johnny crazy, despite the fact that he was genuinely trying to move on. She also passed him the names of the men she went with, knowing full well he wouldn't be able to resist getting them a beating.

'I gradually found out about that bit,' says Jackie. 'It turned my head completely. I couldn't understand on the one hand why she could be so cruel and get away with it, and on the other hand why so many of these men, most of whom were known to Johnny personally, would risk enraging him by shagging her. They must have got some added sexual kick out of it, given his reputation as a "ringleader of death". I got upset about that quite a lot. I hated the thoughts of men getting beaten within an inch of their lives because Johnny Adair's partner was too horny to behave decently. Some of these "crimes" were reported as sectarian attacks at the time, and I felt like ringing up the newspapers and roaring down the phone, "It wasn't sectarian; it was Gina Crossan not being able to keep her knickers on."'

'She stopped going up to the prison after a few months, but they continued to ring one another. When things were going bad between her and Fuzzy, she tried to bring Johnny back on board because not many people were bothering with her then. I realised what a cat and mouse game it was. He needed me then, and at that time I was madly in love with him, though I was hanging on by my fingertips. Little did I know at that point that it would take years more to actually break me. However, even back then, the anger was building up in me to boiling point. I was doing what he wanted, helping him out in any way I could so he could relax behind bars and have an easy life. Whilst their sick games were going on, his kids were knocking on neighbours' doors looking for jam sandwiches. All those people who later became victims of the big UDA feud in 2000 would have laid their lives on the line for him; taken a bullet in the head for him; they even looked after those kids a lot when Gina started going wild on drugs. He later turned against each and every one of them. That's what's so bizarre about this whole story. He started to turn against people within about a year and a half of going to prison.'

The first feud broke out between the UDA and the UVF in August 2000 and the blame for it, according to the latter organisation, lies squarely with Adair. It started when a UDA band parade on the Shankill degenerated into a street war with the local UVF involving fists, boots, bottles, hammers, knives, and eventually firearms and explosives. The net result in the Lower Shankill was Adair dispatching his units to drive anyone remotely connected with the UVF from the estate. Dozens of families, many with small children, were forcibly expelled from his lair. By the end of the feud that autumn, six men were dead and dozens more wounded. Adair's quest for superiority on the Shankill had only ended with the heartland of loyalism broken in two. The lower end of the road was now effectively cleansed of UVF supporters.

Adair, throughout the feud and beyond it, started to behave more irrationally. There were rumours that his industrial intake of steroids was impairing his judgment, that he was in effect 'losing it'. His wife's associations with other men may also have played a large part in his irrational behaviour, according to Jackie.

'When Gina was knocking about with people, they were the very people that both Johnny and Gina were friends with on the outside, so Johnny began turning on them. He never once made Gina take responsibility for her actions, right the way to the end of their relationship, and no one could fathom that. For instance, there was one woman that they both knew that lived across from Gina, and they started going out socialising together. That girl's boyfriend was in prison with Johnny as well. Some kind of argument ensued and Gina stopped socialising with her. She got put out of the estate as a result. That girl then had no one. There were other friends around the corner from him. Gerry Drumgoole, who lost his legs in an IRA car bomb ultimately, worshipped Johnny, but he ended up getting his house wrecked.

Gina had been spreading lies about his family, saying it was their fault that she had been with another fella and the Drumgooles got the blame for it. I used to say to Johnny, "God created you both, but the devil matched yeas." They were an abnormal couple. I told him over a decade ago that he would end up being alone and that Gina would piss off with "new blood" years younger and he'd be separated from his kids. "Don't be saying that, Jackie. That's rubbish," he'd respond. I wonder if he thinks it's rubbish now, stuck in Troon in Scotland with virtually no supporters and Gina shacked up with a guy 15 years her junior. Johnny just couldn't see the wood for the trees when it came to that woman.

'Things got very much out of control at the tail end of 1994/95. I was also having problems. It was during this phase that Paul Orr got that dreadful beating as well. His legs were so badly smashed up—he had to have a load of pins in them—he was in hospital for months. I remember getting the phone call to say he had been beaten so badly that he almost died. I was fuming. He was a lovely guy. As the person was telling me this news the phone was beeping, so I knew it was Johnny ringing up to see if I had heard. I asked him, "Did you get Paul Orr beaten?" He replied, "Hold on a minute. He was my welfare officer and trusted ally. What the hell was he up to sleeping with Gina?" Paul originally used to go down to her house and give her a few quid on Johnny's instructions, and after a while started sleeping with her. It's amazing looking back that I didn't feel sick about Johnny's behaviour even then, but I was blind. It makes no sense. I was trying to get Johnny's mind to make sense, to help him get sorted. I knew he wasn't coping. He kept apologising for all these acts after the damage was done. I think that after a while Johnny got really fed up with Gina. He lost all interest in protecting her and started playing more games with me. Everybody was talking about it. When she had no one, she instantly wanted him back. He had taken the car off her at this stage and stopped her money, which must have been a blow to her as she often asked him for large amounts. She asked him one time for £40,000 with no explanation as to what it was for and he gave it to her, no questions asked. All he got out of it was a pair of Levis. That's why

I think there's some secret there, some "big hold". At a certain point in time he had lost trust in her and instead he would give me the money if it was something that the kids needed, and I'd buy stuff for them. She would get on to him and say, "I love you. We've been together since we were kids. I only went with those men because I found out you were with Jackie Legs."

'She was constantly throwing her weight around while he was inside, telling everyone that she was Johnny's girl. She went to a club one night in Rathcoole and was chatting up this fella. When she went into the toilets, his girlfriend followed her and threatened Gina, "That's my boyfriend out there. Stay away from him, you tramp." Gina's reply was "Do you know who I am? I'm Johnny Adair's girl." She kept this up even when Johnny and I were trying to make a go of things for real.'

While he was in the Maze Adair still had time, in between trying to build a zoo, ensure that his comrades' sexual tastes were sated and running the odd outside terror campaign, to think about Jackie. Despite the ongoing difficulties of the emotional *ménage à trois*, the climax of being Johnny's earnest partner came for Jackie in November 1994 when she asked him to marry her and he agreed. He immediately ran around the wing at the Maze telling all his friends that he was going to marry Jackie Legs. After months of being harangued about which woman he should choose to spend his life with, most of his prison chums were delighted he had reached any conclusion at all.

'Johnny offered me £1,000 for the engagement ring but I told him I didn't need that much,' says Jackie. 'In the end I bought one for £127 instead that I really liked. I walked around Belfast city centre with my daughter and Johnny's sister searching for the right ring. I was so incredibly happy that day. To me, money wasn't important. I went straight to a phone box and rang him after I got it and before I could even speak, he said, "Love, do you need more money?" He almost sounded disgusted when I told him how cheap it was, but that's the ring that caught my eye and to me, the sentiment was all I needed. He told me he had organised an engagement party for me at the Diamond Bar on Saturday night—it was November at this stage—and that I should buy myself something lovely and sexy to wear. I honestly never felt happier in my entire life. He told me to invite all my friends and that everything was paid for.'

Regardless of war, ceasefires, the prospect of peace, the hope of a political settlement and the possibility that one day soon Johnny Adair might walk free early from the Maze, Jackie's mind was preoccupied with her man. Her engagement party, she believed, was a personal triumph over Gina Adair. She had won her own 'war'—or so she thought. And she even received a 'trophy' that was designed to ensure her loyalty to her new fiancé.

'Gina got wind of this engagement party and sent three of her friends, her surveillance sluts, to watch the proceedings,' Jackie says. 'The drink was flowing and there was a great atmosphere. There were tons of cider and ham sandwiches and all kinds of fancy stuff. People offered me money, but I didn't want anything. I kept saying "Please, this is enough; the party is enough." The only sad part was Johnny was locked behind bars and was missing his own engagement party, but the lads got him pissed inside the Maze that night. He did ring up, though, on the mobile halfway through the night to ask me if I was enjoying myself and I told him I was the happiest woman alive. Towards the end of the night, Winkie Dodds called me up on the stage and presented me with an enormous bouquet of flowers and a wrapped present in front of the entire place. The atmosphere was kicking at this stage as everyone was well oiled. They swarmed around the stage to see my reaction. I opened the package and it was a 12 inch vibrator with a note attached to it. It read: "Make sure you wait until the wee man gets out and use this in the meantime." I laughed and assured them that I would. Everyone clapped and cheered. I will never forget that night'.

It can only be left to speculation what ever happened to this token of loyalty so lovingly presented by Winkie, Adair's former friend now turned enemy. If Adair had sanctioned a vibrator for every supporter who has since been relegated to enemy category, it's apparent that the explicit stock of Belfast's four registered sex shops wouldn't have been sufficient to meet the demand.

05 PRISON LOVE AND DAYLIGHT ROBBERY

At the beginning of 1995, Belfast's most legendary shoplifter was looking for an assistant to help him out as a getaway driver and a bit more. Johnny put my name forward and, sure enough, I was up for it. Little did I know just how professional I had become and how much I would get into it, so that Johnny could dress the part in jail.

Adair gathered together some of his cherished cronies in his cell and, giggling like a court jester, said: "Wait until you see this." He dialled Jackie's number and ordered a UB40 CD and a pair of Firetrap jeans, stipulating that the items had to be at the Maze Prison by 4 p.m. that day. This particular brand of denim delight only came on to the market in 1993, and Adair simply adored them. Satirically, the new-fangled clothing brand claimed to be 'inspired by free thinkers and individuals of urban environments' and displayed a mascot called 'Deadly the Gnome', who was allegedly bombarded with 'twisted thoughts'. It could not have been more fitting. The distinctive if not unusual significance of the fashion statement somehow made Adair feel snug. He was also a major fan of 'No Fear' clothing and Jackie supplied him with plenty of T-shirts and baseball caps with the 'No Fear' logo emblazoned on the front. Adair was evidently a man who liked to wear his public heart on a militaristic sleeve.

'It's obvious why he liked that brand!' Jackie sniggers. 'It backed up his already terrifying reputation: "I am Johnny Adair and I don't feel fear, so watch out." The jeans cost about £90 back then, and he knew damn well I wouldn't buy him jeans without a top to go with them,' Jackie reflects. 'I ran around the town like a lunatic and got the stuff for him in record time, but it took ages to find the CD as it was the 1983 'Labour of Love' album he wanted. I had to try about seven different shops.'

Johnny was desperate to get hold of that particular CD specifically to listen to his favourite track, 'Johnny Too Bad'. Unsurprisingly, his mounting ego identified with the lyric as he pined away in his prison chamber waiting for his trial to begin in September:

Walking down the road
With a pistol in your waist
Johnny you're too bad
Walking down the road
With a rocket in your waist
Johnny you're too bad
(Chorus)

You're just robbin' and stabbin'
And lootin' and shootin'
You're too bad (repeat)

One of these days
When you hear a voice say, 'come'
Where you gonna run to?
One of these days
When you hear a voice say 'come'
where you gonna run to?
(Chorus)

You're gonna run to the rock
For rescue, there'll be no rock
You're gonna run to the rock
For rescue, there'll be no rock

That 'rock' more times than not was Jackie. 'I never stole for Johnny, but I would use the money from goods that I stole to buy him what he wanted. It was only when I got to the Maze that day and gave him the bits and pieces that he said proudly, "I told the lads you'd do it Jackie. I said to them you'd never let me down." I realised what a sport it all was for him. He waved the CD over at some of his mates in the visiting room and yelled, "See, I told you." I don't know what's more sad, the fact that he was so embarrassing or that I was so willing to jump to his every command. Yet I was so in love that even seeing him that pleased would fill me with joy. I'd go to any lengths to satisfy the man at the time.'

It was mid-1995 and Jackie had being seeing Adair for three years. Within that time she had been transformed from a jaded housewife to a compulsive thief, and that was just the day job. At night-time she continued to mix with the cream of Ulster paramilitarism and was a keen drug-user and rabid party-goer. The incessant shop lifting could well have been a symptom of Jackie's mental health at the time, which undoubtedly was deteriorating with each year she clung to Johnny Adair. The theft addict—like the gambler or the alcoholic—is hooked by initially getting 'something for nothing', but invariably pays for it in the end. Jackie would ultimately pay for her brand new hobby, being prosecuted at least three times for shoplifting over the next two years, although it's a marvel she escaped stiffer sentences given some of the activities she got involved in.

'After the second time I got done, I got 18 months' probation and a £200 fine,' she says. 'At first I had to go into the PBNI [Probation Board for Northern Ireland] on a weekly basis. Of course, I knew I had done wrong, but the guy they allocated me was a bit of a nut. He kept asking personal questions. "What made you do these things, Jackie? Were you sexually abused as a child, Jackie? Is there anything askew with your sex life now, Jackie?" I asked him what the hell my sex life had to do with shoplifting? I was immediately assigned another probation officer. She came to my house once a fortnight and I also had to meet her in the city centre, initially on a weekly basis. Well, I think she thought I was a crazed maniac too because I was always shouting at her. So the visits became less frequent, once a month or thereabouts, and after she found out I was connected to Johnny Adair, she just stopped calling. That suited me fine. They just stuck to fining me after that.' It seemed that the mere mention of 'Johnny Adair' in any context could send even the toughest bureaucrat running for the Antrim hills.

Meanwhile, the peace process was crawling along at a snail's pace, but in January that year Taoiseach John Bruton and Tánaiste and Minister for Foreign Affairs Dick Spring steered the first formal meeting with representatives of Sinn Féin. The leader of Fianna Fáil, Bertie Ahern, held a meeting with the Ulster Unionist Party (UUP) at its headquarters in Glengall Street, Belfast, three days later. He also met with SDLP and Sinn Féin members to discuss a passageway to peace and a 56-year-old 'state of emergency' in Ireland was lifted. The Framework Document was published a month later, outlining 'a shared understanding between the British and Irish Governments to assist discussion and negotiation involving the Northern Ireland parties'. Despite wholesale suspicion on both sides, dialogue was on the horizon. It wasn't just a political change; it was inevitably a cultural one, as the two communities, who had by now developed a type of habitual hatred towards each other, were raising second and third generations who were suffering literally inbred ethnic prejudice towards one another. For some, thoughts of 'sorting it out' were totally alien.

More critically, the Framework Document was seen by mainstream unionists as heavily loaded in nationalism's favour as it gave the Republic a greater say in Northern Ireland affairs. This concern permeated into the ranks of loyalist paramilitarism, particularly in rural areas of Ulster. In Portadown, the second most infamous loyalist figure Billy 'King Rat' Wright expressed grave disquiet within the UVF that the document could be the vehicle to roll Ulster into a united Ireland. The seeds of the first major split in loyalism were sown in 1995. Wright made up his mind in that period to set up a rival anti-ceasefire loyalist force. Adair had always admired Wright's militancy and that of the

UVF's Mid Ulster Brigade. The C Company commander would eventually follow Wright's path into schism, a return to violence and ultimately fighting with other loyalists.

'I don't remember the whole peace agreement thing too well because I was far from a feeling of peace in my life at the time,' admits Jackie. 'For me the war was switching from the TV into my living room more and more as time went by. It was also a time when, thanks to Johnny, I got into thieving in a big way. Johnny put my name forward to this guy Geordie, who was a professional shoplifter operating all around the north of Ireland. He was absolutely brilliant at his craft and Johnny thought I could do with a few quid and help Geordie out when he was "at work". I had never done anything like it in my life. I started by driving him around, but he said that I would never learn unless I was out there on the shop floor. So pretty soon I was shop-bound with him and the kick was as instant as crack cocaine is today, except that it didn't seem as dangerous.'

Geordie started Jackie off with a straightforward task, to saunter into Woolworth's with a few plastic bags in her pocket, pick out the blind spot (devoid of cameras) and pile up the goods while he'd collect them into plastic bags, and exit. 'The whole CCTV thing wasn't that widespread at the time in a lot of shops, especially smaller ones in towns and villages,' she says. 'No matter what shop you went into, there were always screened areas away from the prying eyes of the security man.

'We would go to Harry Corry and rob bed clothes; from there to a book shop, and finish off in a record store maybe. We would drive from Belfast to Antrim, from Antrim to Ballymena and then up to the Abbey Centre in Newtownabbey and finish off with a few garages along the way. We went to all the wee places where we knew we could get away with it easily. Ballymena was the best, especially Eason's. Political books sold very well on the black market. We would go in and hover about. The next thing, Geordie would say to me, "Open your bag, open that bloody bag", and drop the books in. Between 1995 and 1998 I shoplifted almost daily. We would make between £200 and £300 each a day in the beginning, but that began to increase rapidly. The only day I didn't go shoplifting was Sunday and that was because I'd be out of my head with drugs on Saturday night, so I needed time to recover.

'At Christmas time we would get toys for the kids, and we would sell them on for next to nothing in loyalist circles, but we would still make a huge profit. The quieter towns were ridiculously easy. Ballymena itself was riddled with those small expensive ornament shops, specialist type retail outlets, and the ornaments were worth £200 to £300 apiece. You would walk about and when no one was looking, just slip the ornament into a bag. Don't forget there were few bar codes used then and the only alarm devices on clothing were for really expensive items like leather coats or suede jackets.'

Northern Ireland is littered with large towns such as Ballymena that have a much smaller population than other main urban centres. It has a population of around 30,000 and a large proportion—over 70 per cent—is Protestant. So, ironically, Jackie and her Robin Hood companion were stealing 'off their own' in effect to aid less well-off Protestants in working-class areas of Belfast. Likewise, on the other side of the underground economy, shopkeepers in republican areas were being asked to sell contraband goods. For some residents who couldn't afford the prices that shops charged, buying goods on the black market was another way of escaping paying duty to the British government. In other words, for both communities involved in these illicit activities, the proceeds other than those going straight to the war effort were being clandestinely channelled back into the pockets of individuals with the necessary skills, experience and networks available to sell on the stolen goods. Even now the police in Northern Ireland seize more counterfeit goods than the other 42 police forces put together in the United Kingdom.

While the standard view is that paramilitaries were mainly involved in the buying and selling of weapons, cigarettes or fuel laundering, other commonplace products are also big business, such as DVDs, shampoo, and even condoms. The global annual trade in counterfeit goods is estimated at between €322 and €374 billion, while in the whole of Ireland proceeds from counterfeiting can reach up to €65 million annually. Even in recent times Operation Pine, an intelligence-driven initiative set up between the Gardaí and the PSNI in 2004, seized CDs worth a staggering €750,000 and DVDs worth up to €3 million. Investigators knew for sure that paramilitaries were involved because some of the goods carried political slogans and sarcastic messages such as 'Piracy Creates Jobs' emblazoned on the back of DVD covers.

'Children's story books, crayons, teddy bears, Christmas cards, felt tip pens—all these items were in demand,' Jackie explains. 'There was also a requirement for other stolen goods such as phone cards and electricity stamps that we could sell on.'

Geordie soon realised that Jackie had an aptitude for thieving and introduced her to some more well-known characters adept at making a living on the black market throughout the tail-end of the Troubles. 'We were constantly dropping around to this fella's house and that fella's house; it was bigger business than I ever realised. We went to see one guy who I was told afterwards was very high up in a disparate organisation. When he heard that I was Johnny Adair's girlfriend he went ballistic. He wasn't a fan of Johnny's. "What are you bringing that mad man's girl into my house for?" he snapped at Geordie. However, when he got to know me he became a very good friend. He was a very decent man.'

The antipathy towards Adair by this individual was commonplace inside organisations like the UVF. Long before the feuds between the two organisations on the Shankill Road, the UVF regarded Adair and his gang as unstable, apolitical and uncontrollable. Adair and his buddies countered by alleging that the UVF was less than enthusiastic about taking the war to the IRA. They were, as Adair often quipped, 'the Peace People'. Beyond the intra-loyalist bitching Jackie's shoplifting got worse and worse and increasingly addictive. By the end of the first year Jackie and Geordie were an almost celebrated team in south and east Belfast and were consistently making up to £500 each per day after the first year.

'I had never done anything like that before,' asserts Jackie. 'I just got into it because I saw it as an easy way to get Johnny the stuff he needed in jail and everything my kids needed too. It was a lot easier than relying on social welfare and the cleaning jobs I had had. For the first time in my life I started to dress really well —designer clothes, the best of everything. Even if it was all bought with fool's gold it didn't matter. Johnny Adair was probably the best dressed prisoner in the Maze during this time. He didn't want for a thing and anything he asked me to get him, I gladly obliged, but I always made sure to pay for his goods in cash.'

Jackie soon graduated to credit card fraud and as it was before the days of 'skimming', where data from a card's magnetic strip is electronically copied on to another card and then used, the only way to obtain credit cards was to rob them. 'People within the movement approached us and asked us if we wanted a bunch of cards at a time,' says Jackie. 'We didn't ask where they came from, but the idea was that we would buy them in bulk at a reduced fee and go on a spending spree before their owners woke up to the fact that they had been robbed. I had to learn a few new scams like how to remove the signature from the back of a credit card by using oil on a cotton bud and slowly running it over the signature; it comes clear off. Then you can put your own signature on it.'

Jackie's one and only TV appearance was on *Crimecall* in Belfast in the mid-1990s. The RTÉ flagship crime programme focuses on real crime reconstructions alongside news stories and topical features. Her spurious acting role saw her shiftily buying goods with a counterfeit credit card, wishing the shopkeeper good day and exiting pronto. 'I got a phone call from a friend to say that I was on the TV. I thought she was joking so I didn't even turn it on. Nothing ever came of it. Meanwhile, I had branched out a bit and started operating with another pal, who also hung about with paramilitaries. We used to go around all the garages in Belfast and beyond. We were careful, though, for if there's a limit on a card you obviously can't afford to go over that limit. At that time a lot of garages had those old hand-held machines for processing cards that didn't connect to the banks. We targeted them specifically and would get petrol, cigarettes and the whole shebang. People would also pay us to take their cars to the garages and fill them with petrol, and we would charge them half the cost. It was a great saving for them. The cupboards at home were bunged full with everything—200 cigarettes from this garage, another 400 from that garage, boxes of chocolates, booze, the best of everything really.'

Before long the veritable crime co-operative made its way to Dublin and its larger retail stores. 'We had planned to do a half day in Roche's Stores and Clery's,' says Jackie. 'We stopped at Bridgend on our way. When I went into any place, be it a garage or a shop, I would automatically eyeball for cameras; this day I forgot. My friend and I went in, got petrol and phone cards, signed for the transaction and thought no more about it. We got to Dublin, headed into Roche's Stores and picked up a lot of stuff. All of a sudden we realised we were being followed. I said to my friend, "Get the fuck out; we're being followed." By the time we got out to the car park, there were half a dozen security guards yapping on their radios and running about the place. I don't know how I got out of there, but it might have had something to do with the security guards all being grossly overweight and not being able to run fast. I zoomed past them so fast that one guy had to jump out of the way. My friend started throwing all the clothes we nicked out of the window, panicking. If we had been found with the goods in the car, we would have been locked up in the Republic. You have to pay your bail before you leave a prison in the South; we would have been fucked. It took us five hours to get back we were panicking that much.

If Adair knew that she was robbing in the Republic he would surely have been tickled—his mistress taking her own private war to the heart of the enemy. Jackie soon made approaches to other people to take part in more robberies, a bit higher up the scale again. By this stage she was doing it simply for the thrill as her house that she lived in at that time—Boundary Way in the Shankill—wanted for nothing. Such was her overspill of cash that she got into the habit of doing her house up every six months or so. 'I had so much cash at one stage that I'd get a new settee every few months when I got bored with the old one. I was always very house proud and still am.

'The strange thing was I kept all this pretty much to myself. I've never been much of a blabbermouth. Yet slowly and surely some UDA members got to hear about my antics. John White used to stop me in the street sometimes and say, "Have you got anything for us, Jackie?" He knew what I was up to. He got word that I had been scouting around post offices. I was put in touch with this bloke who did high-flying robberies, but to be honest it all got a bit weird. He became madly obsessed with me but I couldn't take him seriously; my heart was elsewhere. I went on a few jobs with him, just to help out. I didn't know if I had the balls to do it, but I said I'd ease myself in and act as a getaway driver for him. I could drive better than any man could at the time. I was getaway driver for quite a few episodes. Of course, this all got very exciting very quickly, and I wanted more.'

For good reasons Jackie declined to offer comprehensive details, except to say that, like a lot of paramilitaries who resisted the temptation to take school seriously during their younger years, it didn't stop her from taking her 'homework' seriously as an adult in the school of life.

'If, for instance, and now I'm speaking metaphorically here, an individual wanted to rob a post office, this is how they might go about it: they'd stake out the premises and follow the person who opens the shop to their home to see what their routine is. If you know where they live and what car they drive, obviously you can use this to threaten them when you arrive at the premises. They have no way of knowing if you have members of their family detained or not; not many people can afford to take that risk. "Who's in your house?" The person may answer, my mum and my brother or whatever, and then the raiders would say, "Yeah, we know that already; we have two people holding them right now and one of them has a gun", and they'd name the road and house number to verify the information. On both sides of the fence, the tendency was for each organisation to blame the other, so it might be put to the person that when the police came along, to tell them it was the IRA who carried out the heist. Later on that night you could well hear a news bulletin on the TV: "Three masked IRA men held up a post office in . . ." The other side often did the same to us.'

Jackie continued, 'Maybe the raiders would go to a premises at 7 a.m., confront the person and tell them that they're going to walk calmly into the post office with one of the three raiders. The person would have to put the key in the door by half past eight, because that triggers the first alarm to allow entry into the safe. At 8.45 a.m. there is generally another alarm that must be switched on to trigger the next setting. By 9 a.m., yet another button would be activated and then it's a clear pathway to the money. Unless that sequence was followed, an alarm would go off at the local police station,' she explains. 'It would help to do it quickly because there could be old biddies and what not queuing up for their pensions and stuff outside, and you don't want to be upsetting them. If a raider wanted to do a job "decently", they would advise the person they were holding up that if they put in a claim for trauma they'd be entitled to get a few quid back from the government. It was crucial that no one got hurt. The insurance companies make way too much profit ripping people off anyway, let's face it.'

High-level robberies would not just net cash, but also thousands of pounds worth of electricity cards, telephone stamps and other untraceable items that can be sold or given to punters for free. Both republican and loyalist groups—regardless of how much they claim otherwise—partook in stick-ups throughout the Troubles. Even after the Good Friday Agreement and well into the new millennium large-scale heists continued, as is now known with the Northern Bank robbery of 2005, the single biggest cash robbery in Irish history.

'I stopped all the robbing and all that malarkey one day when my then 17-year-old daughter ran up the path of the house screaming, "You robbed that fucking post office this morning, mum, didn't you? Don't try and deny it." I couldn't believe my own daughter thought I was responsible for something she had heard on the news that day. It wasn't her fault; she had after all discovered bundles of cash stuffed in cushions in the house and behind the couch or hidden alongside tins of tomatoes in the cupboard above the cooker. It had reached a stage where my own kids wouldn't put anything past me. I had two teenagers, but I was the one bringing the police to the door and they were running around keeping me in check. On days like that when you realise things are perhaps a little bit distorted, maybe it's time for some life changes. So I went back to ordinary work after that. Don't forget, I was the same person who only four years before would have dashed to the post office in Birmingham to get my TV licence in mortal fear of the licence man calling around. I had gone from bored housewife to an adrenalin-addicted robber inside a few short years. I can't blame Johnny Adair for that, in spite of how crazy he drove me. He did bring the madness out in me, but in reality I seemed to find my way from sanity to lunacy perfectly fine on my own.'

However, Jackie also did a fair bit of unpaid voluntary work throughout her spell as a thief and, indeed, all the way through her rocky relationship with Adair. She helped out regularly at an Alzheimer's centre in Belfast and took pride in comforting patients who weren't visited regularly by their families. 'You hear about that disease all the time, but no one has any idea how heartbreaking it is and how painfully confused a person with Alzheimer's becomes,' she says. 'I used to sit with one old man who was totally convinced I was his wife in the midst of World War II. At first I didn't know how to react but then I thought, sure, if I can give him some comfort, why not? So I'd play along and tell him the Germans would be defeated any day now and we'd be able to eat like lords when they did away with the rations. He'd listen intently and smile and hold my hand. I told him we'd move to Brighton as soon as the war was over and live in a big old house on the seafront. He really liked the idea of that. I was by his bedside the night he died.'

Jackie also single-handedly parented the child of a local drug-dealing couple who were kicked out of the Shankill by Adair's henchmen for anti-social behaviour. 'The child, a little lad just weeks old, was so gorgeous and so lost I couldn't bear the thoughts of him going off with them. As luck would have it, the couple decided it was best to leave the baby with me. He stayed with me for over a year and I looked after him. Actually, when Johnny did get out a few times on parole, he was desperately jealous of the baby and the attention I gave him, which was totally hypocritical as he had young kids of his own that I also looked after. That wee baby brought me a lot of comfort throughout that entire time, as it was during the era when Johnny was losing his head inside the Maze and trying to demolish my sanity. The baby's parents did come and take him back eventually and obviously I didn't have much say in that, though it broke my heart. I would have raised that child to adulthood, no problem.' She also took in two nieces when they were having problems at home. They live in Belfast to this day and Jackie has never been forgiven by her sibling, a situation that still causes her some anguish.

By September 1995, Adair had made up his mind to plead guilty but remained full of beans and waved with enthusiasm at his trusted comrades in Court No. 1 at Belfast Crown Court. Jackie was also there (Gina gave it a miss) and was pleased to see he was wearing the pink silk shirt she had bought him for the occasion. There were also the expected smiles and sniggers to his supporters from the dock. No one beyond C Company appeared to get the joke.

'He wanted to look well for the big day. So I went out and bought him a pink shirt with a stripe through it—he chose to wear that one when he went down officially—but I bought him a range to choose from,' she recalls. 'He was quite calm in the courtroom but you never knew what he was actually feeling.'

A huge influence in securing the charge of 'directing terrorism' was of course down to Detective Sergeant Jonty Brown, who had been a welcome caller at Adair's house for the previous two years, stopping by intermittently for pots of tea and casual chit-chat. Brown would scribble down the details of their chat and weigh it against crime incidents that had remained unsolved. Adair divulged the kind of detail that only a person with personal knowledge of paramilitary manoeuvres could have known. At the point of being sentenced to 16 years for overseeing a regime of terror, he snarled from the dock that his men would 'get Brown', although what he was saying could have added yet more years to his stretch.

'There was a huge crowd there,' reiterates Jackie. 'Johnny's eyes were everywhere; he has shifty eyes anyway. But he was frantically looking around for familiar faces. Two of his sisters were there and his mum. I said to his mum, "I know you don't like me, but all I'm saying is I'm prepared to stand by him." The poor woman seemed very distracted. Unbelievably, there was a woman to the left of me who leaned across to her friend and said, "I'd love to shag him." I told her to shut up or she'd get a slap. I couldn't believe how insensitive that was.'

Probably the most famed citation from the court that day came from the prosecuting lawyer Pat Lynch, who solemnly commented that Adair was 'dedicated to his cause, which was nakedly sectarian in its hatred of those it regarded as militant republicans, among whom he had lumped almost the entire Catholic population'.

'I was very upset the entire time; it seemed unreal,' says Jackie. 'He was totally convinced if he didn't plead guilty they would give him 30 years. He had said to me that week that I should move on and get someone else, that he was going to be incarcerated for a very long time. "A bird like you could get any man," he said, but I told him I didn't care, I was prepared to stand by him. I was dazed when I heard the verdict. I jumped up and roared as loud as I could, "I'll wait for you, Johnny. I love you." But he didn't even hear me. Outside I was dizzy and one of his sisters hit me on the face with an umbrella, screaming, "What are you doing here, you bastard face?" I dropped my head and tears filled my eyes. I just walked off on my own. It broke my heart. I went home and sat on the couch for five hours, speechless. Johnny was gone. He was really gone for good.'

Soon after, Gina made plans to move to Ballynahinch with her current sweetheart, Fuzzy. Johnny subsequently asked Jackie if she wanted to move into the house in Hazelfield Street. The Northern Ireland Housing Executive (NIHE) initially declined

Jackie's request for a public property switch, but when it became clear it was Johnny Adair's house she wanted to move into, they were miraculously accommodating, literally.

'I went around there to have a look at their house,' she recollects. 'It was really beautiful, done up to the nines with every conceivable comfort and gadget inside. He told Gina he'd give her £1,500 to help her start off again elsewhere. By this time I was a "lovely girl" in her eyes as I had been baby-sitting for them and she was quite friendly. "I think I made a mistake about her, Johnny," Gina told him. I was in the hairdressers getting my hair done, and my daughter rang to tell me to ring Johnny urgently. He asked me to drop up some money to Gina quickly so she could hire a car to move her stuff. When I got there Gina said, "You're too late, Legs." I apologised and explained that I had been getting my hair permed and was delayed. That night I drove up to Johnny's sister, Jeanie. She lived in Manor Street. She wanted me to drive her to the Diamond Bar to get a carry-out. When we went in, a friend of Johnny's, Jerry, was there and he said to me, "I hear you're moving into Hazelfield Street. Just a word of warning: you'd want to watch yourself as we'll report everything to Johnny." Jeanie obviously reported back to Gina what had been said, and by the time I got home Johnny was on the phone, fuming.

"What the fuck are you running around saying your Johnny's girl?" he roared. I started crying as I couldn't calm him down. Whatever the guy had said to him about me, Johnny took it to heart. He summoned me to the jail the next day and slammed down the phone. I didn't sleep a wink that night. I nervously waited outside the Maze early the following morning. I made my way into the visiting room, scared stiff thinking of the mood he'd be in. At that time I still didn't answer him back as such; that came much later when they had both wrecked my head completely. So at this time I was still quite docile with him. Johnny looked really annoyed. "Gina said . . ." I stopped him in his tracks. "What is she doing causing trouble for us at this late stage?" I asked him. "I don't care what Gina said about anything. She's gone." He was accusing me of being with people and so on, adding that Gina would never lie to him. I was utterly shell-shocked; she lied to him all the time and everyone knew it. He told me I wasn't moving into his house, ever, and to "cop on and fuck off". He eventually calmed down, but some amount of damage was done. I was desperately hurt and annoyed that he could be that gullible. This professed "director of terrorism" couldn't even direct the traffic, never mind his personal life. I rang Gina when I got home and asked her if she was all right. She seemed really happy. "I've met the man I truly love, Jackie," she said. To this day I believe that. I apologised to her about the entire thing and told her truthfully that I never meant to hurt anybody and that I would be sure to look after her man.'

As the decree of karma would have it, things began to get calamitous for Gina once again. Fuzzy decided he didn't want to go ahead with the move and backed out entirely. It's possible he was afraid of retribution, but either way Gina began to suck up to her estranged partner, Adair, once again, but for the time being her efforts were spurned. She would have to earn her way back into the terror boss's hard-boiled heart. Gina used the kids to fulfil her designs. As Christmas approached, the war of words with the Terrible Three got shoddier.

'There were phone calls back and forth between the three of us all the time because Johnny was increasingly asking me to do things for his kids, now that he didn't trust Gina,' says Jackie. He didn't trust her with money. A few weeks before, he had given her £50 to get Natalie a pair of trainers, but Gina took £40 for herself and gave the kid £10. Natalie was very upset. Johnny hated his kids being upset in any way and felt very out of control being away from them, so when he began to give me the cash to get his kids presents, Gina took offence, naturally enough. I took them to see Johnny on Christmas Eve. It was desperately sad to see all those dads, republicans included, who were going to be without their families for Christmas. The visiting room had an uneasy silence that day, except for the excited chatter of the kids who didn't really understand what was going on. Johnny had tears in his eyes as I led the kids back to the bus.

'Later on that night, he rang to say Gina couldn't put together

Chloe's new electric bike and would I head around there and help out. Like an idiot, I was only too happy to oblige. When I got home, Johnny was on the phone again and he was very down. I made the mistake of telling him that Gina's boyfriend phoned when I was at the house, and he couldn't wait to get off the phone quickly enough to ear bash her. Then, of course, she rang me and called me a bitch. This was how it went on, around and around in loops of menace and madness.

'He rang on Christmas morning and was excruciatingly depressed. He said Gina had set a place for him at the table and got all the kids to say "Happy Christmas" to daddy. This was the way she went on, terrorising the terrorist. He phoned again an hour later snivelling uncontrollably. Gina had put Chloe on the phone; she was only 2 at the time, and got her to put this talking doll on that said mama, dada. "Jackie, why would she do that to me, why? That wee girl clear broke my heart." I told him not to ring back, that it was all getting a bit ridiculous and he was ruining my Christmas. A friend of mine was around at Gina's where there was a load of people drinking away. They were laughing at Johnny ringing up all the time and cracking jokes about Santa getting pissed with the republicans in Dublin and not making it to the loyalist wings of the Maze that year.'

The rabid co-dependency was hurtling out of orbit as active service Romeo and the two Juliets-in-waiting became more embroiled in each other's daily lives and emotions. Jackie maintains that she changed her telephone number over 20 times during this period of ill-treatment, but Adair had an 'insider' in British Telecom who got him phone numbers at the drop of a hat. He had purportedly used this source as part of his intricate intelligence gathering missions for 'jobs'. It meant that Jackie couldn't get away from the situation even when she tried. 'I used to pull the phone out of the wall, but as soon as I plugged it back in at 9 a.m. it would buzz immediately. I just couldn't see that his behaviour was a form of mental bullying. I was incapable of seeing it for what it was because I couldn't let go. I was taking abusive phone calls from Gina as well as Johnny, and my mind was unravelling. She actually rang me one time and accused me of scratching her car at the jail car park. "Wait until I tell you, Gina. I'll drop a breeze block on your head no problem if you'd like to call around to my house now", I told her. It was getting to the stage where I was having really strong fantasies about killing her. I had the spot picked out where I'd bury the bitch and I asked a bent friend of mine where I could get a bag of lime on the cheap.'

It was at this time that Jackie developed another outlandish and arguably eccentric coping mechanism to counteract the abuse. She began writing camouflaged hate-mail to Johnny in jail. She knew 'inside information' about some high profile 'situations' that had occurred years before (although to this day she maintains she'll take this information to her grave and would never be 'that disloyal' to Johnny) and began taunting him by Royal Mail. What she was powerless to do in her waking life she began to pen down furiously in the hope that she would drive him over the edge with paranoia. She carried on sending him the letters for three years.

'It got to the stage where if he'd had the balls to kill himself, I think I would have run through Belfast naked to celebrate,' she declares. 'He was telling me what Gina was doing to him and I was listening to what he was doing to her about what she was doing to me. I became dreadfully stressed out all the time and got hooked on Diazepam (Valium). My reasoning was clear; the more I took the less I'd feel. I would take half a dozen at night before bed and as soon as I woke up I would have to take another handful. I lost track of how many I was taking because I was getting them illegally and there was an endless supply. Not only that, I had a son and a daughter and I wasn't there for them. I completely neglected them. I should have been there for them, but instead they were watching me destroy myself. I still live with the guilt of that.'

Gina phoned Jackie towards New Year and asked her would she have the kids on the 31st. Jonathan, the eldest who was 11 years old, was meant to stay with Jackie that night but asked instead if he could stay over at a friend's house near by. Gina was out at the Alexander Bar on the Shore Road enjoying some drinks with

friends. At 4 a.m. Johnny rang Jackie in total turmoil, saying that
a man had tried to rape Gina in their Hazelfield Street home.
Seemingly, the guy had followed her there and attacked her in the
bedroom.

'She was seen chatting away to this bloke, Abby, in the bar and
they left together and got into a taxi,' assesses Jackie. 'Gina
popped in to see some mutual friends who lived a few doors away
to say "Happy New Year" on her own and headed home. It seems
it was an alibi. Unbeknownst to her, Jonathan had decided to
leave his friend's house and went home. He wandered in and
caught them in the act, and Abby shouted at him to get lost. It
seems fairly obvious what really happened. The next day the UDA
in west Belfast called a meeting and this guy Abby was going to be
shot for this "attack". He was supposed to be picked up at 2 p.m.
that day and done away with. I was so upset and couldn't let it
happen. I jumped into the car at 1 p.m. and drove as fast as I could
to Winkie Dodds' house. He wasn't in so I headed straight for the
UDA headquarters in the Shankill. I desperately tried to convince
Dodds and White as to what I thought happened and begged
them to spare the life of this man. So it was agreed, and instead
he got a few slaps about the head. Of course there was an
immediate reprisal for me, and a day or so later Johnny rang
screaming like a mad man down the phone accusing me of being
with some fella and said that Gina told him. If the truth be told,
he really thought he "owned" both of us.'

The crunch came just two weeks later when Gina's sister asked
Jackie to run her up to the jail one Saturday morning. Unaware
that Gina had given her sister a package to give to Johnny, Jackie
obliged and darted up to the Maze. 'I got a phone call at 10 o'clock
that night. "Gina wants me back, Jackie." I couldn't understand
what had changed. She had sent him a letter and a Celine Dion
CD with the song, "Think Twice". "Jackie, my head is telling me
you, my heart is telling me her." I got the feeling he wanted me to
talk him out of it because he kept saying that no one had ever
loved him like me; that I made him feel like a real person.
However, Gina took over the prison visits once again since the
first time he had been sentenced (she hadn't been to the jail since

the previous September) and he bought her a blue Escort as a type of "back on again" present, and that was that.'

A verse of the song carried a poignant forewarning for Gina:

> Don't say what you're about to say.
> Look back before you leave my life.
> Be sure before you close that door,
> before you roll those dice.
> Baby think twice.

That was enough to make 'Baby' Adair 'think twice' and he jumped clear from the deck of the love boat, yet again. Incredibly, a hackneyed chart song was enough to fine-tune the terror chief's reasoning to another frequency. But instead of leaving Jackie alone to flounder in her heartache, he continued ringing her at all hours of the night asking her if she thought he had made the right decision by dumping her! 'In between his calls Gina would also be ringing me,' she recalls. 'I pleaded with her not to speak ill of me, and she thanked me for being there for Johnny when she wasn't.'

Six weeks later Adair was back on the phone to Jackie, begging her to come to the jail once again, adding that he had something to explain. When she got there he said that Gina was up to her old tricks again and would she start seeing him again. 'And what did I do?' enquires Jackie. 'I went back to the asshole.'

However, this time there would be a major variation in the game plan. Jackie was soon to become the first woman at the Maze to be granted coveted sex sessions with her lover via 'closed visits', despite not being his legitimate partner. 'He was harping on continuously about how sexually frustrated he was and that he desperately needed a "good ride". I thought it might do us both good and told him to apply to the governor for a "private visit", to tell the prison authorities that he was having dire problems in his personal life—which was true—and that he needed to sort it out. I had a feeling that they would give him anything he wanted, if only to avoid a riot. Johnny Adair would trigger trouble in jail if his sex life relied on it. So that's what was organised.'

It was totally unheard of at the time, but given Adair's reputation, Jackie knew it was possible. He couldn't stop talking about it. "Christ, I'd love to have sex, Jack. It's been a long while, you know," he said. Gina had split up with him at this stage and Jackie was his 'partner' of sorts at the ready. Adair immediately snitched to all his mates what was on the cards after he applied to the governor for the hush-hush bonking session. They thought he was once again indulging in the hazardous waste of make-believe. But they were wrong.

There was also a serious side to Jackie's request. 'I desperately wanted his child. I think in hindsight I wanted something permanent from him because I was that much in love and I knew I couldn't have him, so I wanted the baby,' she admits. 'I know that's irrational, but there it was. We talked about having a child and he wasn't against the idea. Johnny had been tricked into having a child before with a woman so he was very reluctant to try for a child with me. But I don't believe in tricking men in that way so I carried on taking my pill faithfully. I didn't want to go for it unless he really wanted to. We did agree to try, and would have a stab at it for six years or so. I don't know if it was God's will, or if the steroids he took had anything to do with it, but it never happened.'

When the day arrived, Jackie was under strict instructions as to what to wear: a short black skirt (with no panties underneath), a pair of long black boots and a figure-hugging top (he didn't mind what colour). 'I was so excited, I just couldn't wait,' Jackie says. 'This was the perfect thing to get us back close, to get rid of all the emotional abuse and just allow us to feel truly intimate again. When a man is locked up in jail like that, he's lacking a female touch. I missed that intimacy with him and I knew it would sort him out. My main objective was always to please Johnny. You get to a man not through his stomach, but through his dick; any woman who's been on this planet long enough knows that. I knew when I got my hands on him physically we'd feel different towards each other.

'I strolled into the room where they search you and gave myself up to the woman as usual. When I got the all clear, I went into the toilet and took my knickers off and put them in my pocket before heading on up to see Johnny. Two male prison officers led me into a tiny room at the very end of one corridor and told me to wait for a few minutes. From their smirking it was clear to me that they knew exactly what was happening. When Johnny came in, his face was a total picture. He was beaming, holding a tin of coke, but his hands were actually shaking with anticipation. "Are you all right then, Jackie?" he asked. In reality we were both quite nervous to start with.

'The room was quite bleak and bare, not the type of place you would ever imagine making love in, but he got so excited he knocked the can of coke clear off the table and sent it flying across the room. "Sorry!" he sniggered, and I told him to walk over to me, that we didn't have long and what kind of man was he to be keeping a scorching hot woman waiting for her prize. He stood in front of me and I could see his breath fill the air, but I wasn't in the mood for wasting any time. I unzipped him, bent down and immediately gave him oral pleasure. He let out a loud gasp and I could hear the prison officers laughing, but I didn't want to lose my concentration. To be honest, I thought he was going to explode there and then. He could hardly contain himself. It had been a long time since he'd had full-blown sex. He quickly got very animalistic and threw me over the small table and reefed up my skirt. He was quite selfish about it, but I understood and I didn't mind. To me, it was enough that he was getting the level of satisfaction he so desperately needed. When he finished he held me close and we both shook a bit. I left and the two prison officers said, "Bye now. Take it easy." But I was too pleased with myself to bother answering. I floated out of the prison. When I got back to the house, the phone was ringing as I put the key in the door. "Oh Jackie, that was bloody mega!" he said. "Here, wait till I tell ye. All the lads are demanding these closed visits now and that's down to you, love!"'

It might not make the history books or even go down as a focal point in the midst of a new-born peace process, but there was a point in time in 1996 when the Maze Prison became a paramilitary rabbit warren, bobbing up and down to the beat of

Johnny Adair's famished libido. Yet, despite the raucous sex and the rehabilitated promises of a glorious future with Jackie, Johnny Adair married Gina Crossan at the Maze on 21 February 1997, complete with vodka-filled balloons to send them on their way to 'till death do us part'. Naturally, Adair rang Jackie straight after the ceremony had ended and was desperate for her counsel. His face had apparently broken out in a nasty rash. "Jackie, did I do the right thing, did I, did I, did I?"

06 | I'M NO WHORE, JOHNNY!

At the doctor's surgery I spotted a pregnant woman, the wife of another top loyalist who also had a full-time mistress. I realised all these men were not just doing a good job of screwing up the country but were screwing up their women as well. I started roaring, 'I'm going to kill that bitch Gina Adair!' Within ten minutes they had dragged me off to the nut house.

There are 35 beds in Windsor House and Jackie maintains by the time she got there she had a disorder for every bed in the ward. When she collapsed at her doctor's surgery, she weighed less than six and a half stone and hadn't slept for four months. The psychiatric unit, based in the grounds of Belfast City Hospital, admitted Jackie after her doctor classed her as an 'emergency case'. When the acute in-patient team gathered around her bed to have an initial chat with her, she told them out straight. 'I want my pound of flesh. I'm going to murder that fucker Gina Adair and I'm going to burn her body till it's black and stinking like a scorched rasher.' They walked off perplexed. The initial assessment hadn't lasted long at all—yes, Jackie Robinson was undeniably having a nervous breakdown.

Windsor House deals with all manner of mental illness from anxiety and depression to conditions including schizophrenia and bipolar disorder. Staff members are used to seeing people in the abysmal shape Jackie was in that day when her entire physical and mental system plunged into acute overload. The advent of a nervous breakdown is always the result of chronic and unrelenting nervous strain and not a sign of weakness in the person. Like any machine, the human body will start to malfunction when put under too much stress and nervous strain.

'You know what you're doing and you're trying to get to the top, but the more you claw to get there, the further you sink,' describes Jackie. 'It's the poxiest feeling in the world; you're totally remote. You fear the pain the whole time you sense it near, but when you're eaten by it you don't want to move ever again because the thought of coming back into life is too terrifying. Death wouldn't have been enough for me. Only people who truly love you can tow you back from that kind of torment because you're completely unable to help yourself. Without love you'd be fucked. My kids and my sister Kim brought me back to life; they resuscitated me in the end.'

Jackie's description of nervous collapse is terrifying. She felt she had been shoved past human borders and was (for a while) living somewhere else wholly unrecognisable. She could hear animals, engines, snippets of conversations from when she was a child. She couldn't rid the image of swans from her head—'I loved them when I was a kid; they're so graceful, my favourite animal in the world'—and at one stage, curled tense in a ball, unable to move in the middle of the bed, she felt stiff and inert like a scone left to go cold on a blistered cooking tray. 'I had gone, left the world,' she confesses. 'I don't even understand that place where I was when I think back on it now. I really pity people with mental illness, to be stuck in that stinking hell for years at a time. I'd top myself, no question about it.'

Like anyone in the grip of acute psychosis, it goes without saying that privacy and rest are fundamental to recovery, no visitors for the first few days, no phone calls, no interference of any kind. The unit itself does not allow unvetted personal calls to patients admitted in acute states. But medical science doesn't apply to Johnny Adair. Within ten minutes (no one knows how) he got wind of what happened, where she was, the telephone number of the unit, and managed to outfox the reception desk and catch his mistress unawares. 'There's a phone call for you,' the nurse whispered, strolling out with Jackie, holding her bony arms and jutted elbows. 'Jackie, it's me, it's Johnny. What the fuck? Jackie, are you OK? Fuck'n hell, Jackie, this is my fault. Is this my fault? Is this down to me, Jackie, is it?"

'You know those weird 1950s arty films, the black and white ones where nothing happens for the first two minutes or so,' she says. 'There might be a bloke in an American diner wiping tables and all you can hear is the buzzing noise of the fan above him, and after a while he bashes the fuck out of a fly and squashes him on the wall, and then the film starts. Well, I was that fly; he was the buzzing noise. When I heard his voice, I just slid along the wall as if I was made of slime, right down to the floor and flopped all over the place, dropping the receiver as I went. That's all I remember; the rest is a blank. I was there for five days in total, sedated to the eye balls, and that's all I remember.'

Jackie can't even describe the place today because she has virtually no memory of it. 'I think it was one big room, white walls, clinical, you know, with people sitting around pissing themselves and talking away on their own and stuff like that. I think there were locks on the doors. I just can't remember, to be honest. They medicated me to knock me out for a proper rest as I hadn't slept for so long. No one really spoke to me there. I found out afterwards that I was actually in "no fit state" for counselling, so I just slept with my eyes open. I do remember my sister Kim being there at one point trying to settle me down, and my daughter trying not to cry. When I lost it in the doctor's surgery that day, the doctor did say to me, "You are capable of what you are saying and I'm worried that you're a danger to yourself and others." I was totally serious about killing Gina. I had been pushed over the edge and was refusing to land. In my madness I felt I was entitled to do anything I wanted and get away with it. I was so demented I felt justified in committing murder. I felt I could explain it to a judge and he'd nod and say, oh yes, now I see what you're saying. No problem, this court is adjourned. I've no idea how Johnny got the number and the information so quickly that I was there. It goes to show the type of intelligence he had—

and probably still has.'

For weeks she was treated for depression with Valium and heavy-duty anti-depressants. 'Actually when I think about it now, it's fucked up in more ways than one,' she claims. 'My doctor wanted my daughter to get me electric shock treatment which was a hell of a responsibility to put on a kid her age, and obviously the thought of it scared her. She and my son thought I was losing it because I was drinking too much. As I slid further downhill, I tried to hide a lot from them or at least I thought I had. Eventually my daughter and sister came to take me home. They didn't feel that lying there was doing me much good. My daughter agreed with my sister that she would look after me. God love her, she was only 16 years old and was lifting me in and out of the bath; I hadn't the strength to even wash myself. I hate the thought that I did that to her now. She was too young to be minding me in that kind of way. A decade later and she's still very protective towards me. How can I ever make that up to her?'

When Jackie signed herself out she changed her telephone number and headed to England to her mum for a rest. She felt if she got away, even for a few weeks, she would gather enough strength to turn from Adair for good. 'A month later, my daughter went to visit my mum in Birmingham for a holiday. She desperately needed a break, God love her. When she came back, she flung a load of photographs down on the table, photos of her trip and some that my mother gave her. There was a picture of this grotesque ugly woman that she gave me and she started to cry. "Oh my God," I cried, "what's wrong, love?" She was blubbing, "Mum, that's you." I didn't even recognise myself from my trip four weeks ago. The face was sharp like a knife it was that thin, chin all pointed, eyes bulging, loose skin. I actually looked like some kind of mental puppet. "That's not me!" I said, kind of amused at first, but when I sat and really looked at it, I cried my heart out. You just don't realise how bad you are, how bad you look when you're inside that body that's deteriorating. I posted it to Johnny with a note, "This is what you've done to me." But really I had done it to myself, hadn't I? He rang me and asked why I'd sent it. He seemed disinterested, annoyed even, although I fooled myself that he cared. Maybe he did in his own weird way.'

Instead of boycotting the frying pan, Jackie nosedived back in, heading to the Maze to see a friend of hers only a week later, knowing she'd bump into Johnny. 'When he saw me, he jumped over the barrier and came straight over,' she remembers. "Jackie, you look dreadful," he whispered. "Did I do this to you?" And he genuinely seemed upset. He held me there for a while and I felt like papier maché in his arms. He was so used to being looked after and fussed over I really don't think he knew how to look after someone else.'

According to Jackie, Adair couldn't see that he had put himself in jail, even years into his sentence. He complained unrelentingly that he was wedged in between a 'load of murderers and perverts'. He saw himself as way above the wanton, gratuitous or nauseous behaviour of other lowly criminals. He had, after all, sorted the IRA out, brought Northern Ireland to its knees, made 'those uns' (politicians) stand up and do something. 'I honestly think if the UDA weren't paying for his phone cards, he would have done himself in,' she says. 'He literally wasn't surviving in jail and needed to ear bash as many people as possible to maintain that link with the outside. He used to be so hurt and confused if someone didn't like him, and he would moan like mad about it. "Why do people say in the papers that I'm a drug dealer, Jackie? It's not fucking true. Why are they saying bad things about me all the time?" Many a time I'd ask him if he wanted me to say that it was all lies, that he really didn't do half those things they [journalists] were accusing him of? He knew I wouldn't lie to him and that I'd always give him the truth, but then he didn't like what he heard. He really was turning into a "no win" merchant as time went by and increasingly paranoid.'

Soon enough, the convention of 'agony aunt' and 'blabbermouth' returned to a type of conformist-normal. Johnny was back surfing the phone lines picking up the waves where they had left off. Things were heating up again politically as well and Johnny felt 'cut off' from what was going on outside. 'I don't think he knew or cared half the time what went on politically,' says Jackie. 'Johnny was a military man through and through; all he cared about was "if they're still popping our blokes, we'll pop twice as many of the fuckers. That's the only language the IRA understands." I don't think he gave a flying fuck about hardcore politics at all.'

At the beginning of 1998, the UFF along with the UDA chose to withdraw their support for the peace process. They expressed fury at the British government's handling of the talks, believing that there was evidence of preferential treatment towards republicans, Sinn Féin and the IRA. While political leaders were insistent that the ceasefire lingered in place, the po-faced world of loyalist paramilitarism was not in the mood for waiting games. From the Maze Prison the leadership of the UDA announced that the loyalist ceasefire was 'extremely fragile'. The UDA prisoners also demanded equal treatment with republicans.

Mo Mowlam, then Secretary of State for Northern Ireland, held meetings with unionist and nationalist politicians at Stormont Castle and would later meet up with Johnny and his crew to convince them to come on board the peace train. The DUP described the decision by Mowlam as madness, while the UUP embraced the move and considered it 'constructive'. Of course she was also going to meet up with republicans at the Maze. The meeting went down well and Johnny was said to be 'visibly moved' afterwards. It was, after all, the first time he had properly met up with 'those uns' and it rid some of his la-di-dah prejudice about politicians 'not having a clue'. He was impressed by Mowlam's attempts to get them to see sense. Johnny began to think that maybe peace was possible.

The UDA in general supported the Good Friday Agreement, as did Adair in the early stages, after all it would lead to Adair's early release (and other prisoners). The problem was the UDA is federal and factional by nature. Other areas were lukewarm. Moreover, Adair fell under the spell of the ghost of Billy Wright (killed at Christmas 1997). Wright and his successors were opposed to any deal with nationalism. This influenced Johnny greatly and led him into a coalition with the LVF, which in turn was manipulated by a gang of self-appointed Protestant pastors who hated any accommodation with Catholics. Strangely, John White remained a supporter of the Good Friday Agreement right to the end. Adair veered between White and Wright. He see-sawed in his support for a peace deal. This was made more erratic due to his intake of steroids and other drugs. By the summer of 2000 he was 'up for anything', including that damaging feud with the UVF, the one that will ultimately sign his fate as the UVF say themselves: 'We have very long memories and infinite patience." The latter is something Johnny was never blessed with. There is an ongoing theory that it will be the UVF who will 'take him out' in the end; those close to Adair even today believe that to be true.

While the LVF continued to kill innocent Catholics during this period of concentrated negotiations, there was some level of let-up from the UFF. There was the odd vicious incident, usually carried out in direct retaliation for one of their own being hit. In January 1998, the same month that Mo Mowlam braved a visit to the Maze, Jim Guiney, a UDA commander from Dunmurry, was shot dead by two members of the INLA. That same day, Larry Brennan, a Catholic civilian, was shot dead by the UFF on the Ormeau Road. The tit-for-tat ogre had not totally disappeared from under the bridge. By the end of January, Ronnie Flanagan, the Chief Constable of the RUC, maintained that the UFF were involved in the 'recent killings of three Catholics' even though they had said they were soldered to a ceasefire indefinitely. The UFF responded that it was looking again at its own tactics and that they would reinstate their ceasefire following a 'measured military response'. It was crucial that the killings should stop; they did not after all want to risk the removal of the UDP from the peace talks. If the IRA were to be taken seriously, then they had no choice but to follow suit.

In fact it was the IRA who put the first foot wrong. In February, Robert Dougan, a chief loyalist, was shot dead in Dunmurry, near Belfast. No organisation claimed responsibility, but the police were convinced it was the work of the IRA and consequently Sinn Féin were kicked out of the multi-party talks, a move that enraged its president, Gerry Adams. It issued a statement to say that the ceasefire was still a reality and they were incorporated into the talks in the end, albeit warily. There was still an element of mistrust around.

'Johnny's head was done in that year,' recalls Jackie. 'He supported the talks one minute but wanted to run out into the garden like a kid with a toy gun and shoot all around him the next. He was incredibly stressed, which meant I was also becoming likewise. He was worried sick the INLA were going to get him, that he'd be the next republican target. "Those bastards won't rest till I'm under [the ground], Jack." After weeks and weeks of phone calls on a daily basis, and normally all night as well, my mind was turning psychopathic again. Even with a very real threat to his life, he was still preoccupied with Gina screwing around. He rang again one day, going on and on about Gina's sexual conquests. My brain was pounding. I slammed down the phone, jumped into the car and drove straight to the UDA offices where I got John White to go to Gina's house with me. She was bullying and terrorising Johnny and it was causing repercussions on the wing where he was driving other prisoners insane about his love life. There was even graffiti on walls in the Maze from other prisoners who'd "had her", and Johnny was becoming increasingly disturbed.'

Gina had by this stage begun ringing Jackie's house and calling her daughter a whore and insulting her son and telling him he would get a beating. Jackie had already 'salvaged' her young son from the UFF 'thumping squad' after rumours were circulated that he was going to get a hiding for anti-social behaviour. The rumours turned out to be totally false. 'My son was and is gentle and not at all bad or nasty,' says Jackie, 'so much so that I'm actually surprised he's turned out the way he has, given what I have put him through. Sham Millar called to my house one day and said that my son was wanted at headquarters and was going to be "dealt with" for anti-social behaviour. Well, I soon put a stop to that. I'd kick the living shit out of any human being that laid a finger on my kids. I would have no qualms about killing them stone dead. It simply wasn't going to happen. I got to the source of the lie and, of course it led back to a certain lady who lived in Manor Street at the time. D-Day had arrived. I wanted John White with me as a witness so that when I kicked the livin' shit out of her, she couldn't twist it any other way like she did before.'

A few months earlier the two love rivals had had it out in the midst of a traffic jam. 'I was dropping a mate to a club in Agnes Street when I heard this horn beep behind me. It was Gina trying to annoy me inside the safe shell of her car. She had an audience of young lads who were standing at the side of the road, including her son Jonathan. I stuck up my fingers at her and she overtook me. I overtook her in return. My friend in the car was getting nervous. "No Jackie, don't get into this, don't." I slammed on the hand-brake when we were both stopped at traffic lights. I ran to Gina's car, pulled the door open and knocked her across to the other side. In my temper, I hit my head off the inside roof and managed to split my eye open. Even with blood squirting everywhere I couldn't stop myself. I had finally lost control. Gina had me by the hair and we were punching the life out of each other. She was screaming, "You leave my husband alone, you psycho bitch." A friend of mine had her arms around my waist trying to drag me out of the car. "What right have you to call me a dirty bastard when you used your husband's money to get rid of another man's baby?" I roared. I told her I'd get her, no matter how long it took me. I heard the day after that she went home and got a knife and called around to loads of houses on the Shankill showing them the blood and saying that she had stabbed and beaten Jackie Legs. And Johnny was apparently proud of her. I think he really got off on the attention the two of us showered on him by being rivals. To him it was all a game. He later told people that Gina kicked the shit out of me. It was total rubbish. She twisted the story completely. I told him years ago: "One day she'll leave you for another man. Mark my words, you'll end up a very lonely and isolated man and she'll come to nothing." That bit has come true even if he is getting his end away in Glasgow band halls on the remnants of his reputation.

'On this particular day, I said to White, "You're coming with me now because I want you there to see what I'm going to do to that bastard." Gerry Drumgoole's wife was in Gina's house at the time; it was clear she found the whole incident amusing—she asked if I wanted a cup of tea! It looked as if Gina was hiding in the bedroom and wouldn't come down the stairs. "Gina get down here now. I'm going to kick the fuck out of you!" I shouted up the stairs. She opened the bedroom door and called down to me to pick up the phone in the sitting room, which I did. It was Johnny. "Jackie, what are you doing getting all psycho on my wife. Please leave the house, if only for the kids' sake." I told him to fuck off and put the phone down. Gina ran back into her bedroom and I howled up the stairs that I'd get her for making a constant fool out of me. This was it; years of abuse were coming to an end right now. White suggested we leave at that point.'

On Friday, 10 April 1998, the Good Friday Agreement was born after a severe and prolonged labour. George Mitchell, chairman of the multi-party talks at Stormont, delivered the historic statement: 'I am pleased to announce that the two governments and the political parties in Northern Ireland have reached agreement.'

Even if both sides grumbled over the fine details, the main points of the Agreement were: a Northern Ireland Assembly with 108 seats, elected by proportional representation; a 12 member Executive committee of ministers to be elected by the Assembly; the setting up of a North-South Ministerial Council within one year by the Assembly, the council being accountable to the Assembly and the Dáil; amendments to Articles 2 and 3 of the Irish Constitution to establish the principle of consent, and the repeal of the British Government of Ireland Act; a Council of the Isles with members drawn from assemblies in England, Scotland, Wales, Belfast and Dublin. It wasn't all glowing on the 'orange' side of the fence. The Grand Orange Lodge, the ruling body of the Orange Order, decided not to support the Good Friday Agreement, but the Ulster Unionist Council (UUC) supported it by a majority vote of 72 per cent within its membership. Needless to say, it didn't pass by without some level of discord. At the end of the day, history had turned whether Johnny liked it, loathed it, or was indifferent.

'Johnny was told by someone that there might be a chance of his early release, even though at first he didn't think the

Agreement and all its "offerings" would include him,' says Jackie. 'He knew by now that the media, the police and the public had it in for him, but he didn't know why. To be honest, his main concern and his main topic of conversation was still Gina's knickers. I often wondered what kind of kinkiness Johnny and Gina had together; they both slept around but would persecute one another about what they did in the sack with other people. Mind games were what those two were best at.'

A Referendum was planned for 22 May which would ratify future changes of the Good Friday Agreement to the Irish Constitution. The United Unionist Campaign (UUC) launched a 'Right to Say No' campaign in Belfast to oppose the Good Friday Agreement in the referendum, urging its followers to opt for a No vote. Sinn Féin, on the other hand, rallied around the Yes stance. This was also backed by Tony Blair, and US President Bill Clinton dispatched a personal message to the people of Northern Ireland calling on them to vote Yes in the forthcoming referendum. In May, just before the Referendum, the LVF announced a ceasefire. It seemed as if all and sundry were taking the path to peace seriously. The day of the referendum arrived, the first all-Ireland poll since the general election of 1918. The turnout was enormous across the island. Northern Ireland voted Yes by a staggering 71.1 per cent, while in the Republic the Yes vote attracted 94.39 per cent. The overall result for the entire island of Ireland was: Yes 85.46, No 14.54 per cent.

One of the immediate after-effects of the Good Friday Agreement was the re-emergence of 'decommissioning' as the political 'soup of the day'. Johnny was excited because even if he wasn't totally confident of being let out of his kennel, he could sense that the change occurring was bona fide, if not sincere. He warbled about living a peaceful life on the outside if/when he got out. He talked to friends about getting a job, leading a normal life and taking it easy with his family. No one paid any attention to his romantic visions of a new Ireland on the Shankill. In keeping with previous habitual behaviour, Jackie maintains that Gina continued to sleep around and use the Johnny Adair-type narcissism as a way to get to men's hearts and underpants the more his name was bandied about the media. 'You know, even when he was thrown back into the slammer in recent years, I still heard these stories long after I stopped seeing Johnny,' she continued. 'Even a recent example of this game playing happened in 2003 when Johnny was lifted off the streets after the feuds with the UVF in the Shankill. Gina lured a [Catholic] man into bed after a night out clubbing. He didn't know her from Adam but wanted to meet up with her again. When he asked her for a contact number she asked him, "Do you know who I am?" He assumed she was taking the piss, so he asked her to explain. "I'm Johnny Adair's wife and he's going to shoot you for sleeping with me." I heard that from a journalist whose mother's house was being painted by this guy a few months later.'

Johnny had been out several times on parole and did his best to keep Gina in check, but he usually ended up creating his own brand of havoc on the streets instead. As far back as 1996, he was given 'compassionate release' to attend his father's funeral. His father Jimmy was widely admired and said to be a lovely man. A pigeon racer all his life with long-standing contacts in west Belfast, he was not at all sectarian. Johnny's mother, as many will verify, adored him and stuck by his every move.

'Before Johnny went to jail, his mother Mabel would get up early and go for the paper most days, and then she'd walk down to Johnny's house and check his car for bombs,' Jackie says. 'His father was a really pleasant man, very down to earth and no bullshit about him. He was well respected in his neighbourhood. I went around there to pay my respects. Gina was in the living room sitting on the couch with her head down. Johnny seemed pleased to see me. His two sisters, Margaret and Mabel were there and I gave them a kiss. I went and stood by the coffin with his mother and I bent over and kissed Jimmy Adair on the head. Johnny came into the room and asked me outside to the back garden, to "see the flowers", so I went out with him. "Are you OK?" I asked him. "Ah, sure what can you say?" he replied. He started to tease me a bit. I had started to see Keith again and he was asking me about all that, but I was careful about how I answered him. It was soon after that that he married Gina.'

Back in jail, Adair had started a kind of reading circle inside his prison cell on Saturday nights. 'I was out having a drink on the Shore Road and this fella came up to me and said, "You've a great knack for writing. I reckon you have a talent there." I had no idea what he was talking about,' says Jackie. 'He told me that Johnny used to gather around a few special friends in his cell on a Saturday night and he would read out my letters which were often quite explicit. When we started having sex in the Maze I began writing him "sexual letters" that were intended for his eyes only, but apparently he and the lads would be breaking their sides laughing at the details of our intimate life together. I felt it was a real betrayal.

'I decided to get my life in order without Johnny, if that was at all possible, even if his calls didn't stop. I would move on alone. I had started seeing this guy called Keith. He gave me such a boost and made me feel good. He was a lovely fellow, very gentle, interesting, and fun, the kind of mixture of things that most women look for. As soon as I made arrangements to see him, Johnny found out and was on the phone immediately. He told me I would be a failure in bed with anyone other than him. His very words were, "Jackie, you'll be a dead ride after me." He was insanely jealous, phoning the house incessantly if Keith was there. All I could do was cry. Keith held me in his arms and calmed me. "Jackie, you've every right to move on. He'll get used to it." But I was already in a panic, "No he won't Keith; you don't understand just how controlling this man is." No one understood. One way he inhibited and controlled me was to turn his own behaviour on me by telling everyone I was obsessed with him and wouldn't stop ringing him. It was, in fact, the other way round. He was by this stage a dysfunctional lunatic riddled with paranoia because of who and what he was and, more importantly, who the public thought he was.

'Keith and I were out one night at a pub in Belfast; he disappeared off to the toilet but was gone quite a while. I could sense that something was wrong and went to look for him. When he came back he looked a bit shaken and asked if we could leave straight away. Some of the "lads" from the Shankill took him into a cubicle and searched him for drugs. They had got word from an unnamed source that he was a drug dealer, which was just pure ridiculous. Keith was as straight as a dye, worked as a tradesman and was probably the only person I knew who was leading a law-abiding life. The blood drained from me when he told me they had warned him that he'd get shot if he showed his face around the area again. I felt sick. I knew who was responsible. I decided to confront these hoods there and then and went back into the pub on my own. I couldn't find the fellas but I did speak to a friend of a friend, a woman who was off her head in the toilets talking to herself in the mirror after downing a load of drugs. "Jackie, that guy there, the big guy you're with, Johnny has told the lads to give him a good beating." I nearly lost my mind. We left and went to the Glencairn shebeen. We both felt uneasy after the experience in the previous place, so I went outside with Keith when he was going to the toilet. It was all very surreal. A guy came up to me and said, "I recognise you. What the hell are you doing with a wanker like Adair?" It was going from one charade to another. A few of the boys who were sitting at the table across from us starting throwing empty cans at Keith, so we decided to leave before it got really heavy.

'Johnny had done all the damage he could think of doing. The next morning I was crying in the kitchen when Keith walked in. I told him there and then he had a choice, to stay or to walk away. He said he would stay. That morning I headed up to a friend of Johnny's in Highfield to try and sort all this out. I enlightened him as to what was going on and he said he'd speak to Johnny for me. Later that afternoon Johnny gave his word that Keith would be left alone and the fictitious drug dealer talk would stop. But Johnny's word was not up to much. Keith's family were understandably worried and appalled that he was seeing a woman connected to Johnny Adair and wanted him to stop seeing me. The whole thing seemed really unjust. I had just recovered from a breakdown and was attempting, slowly, to move on with my life, but Johnny would not permit me to walk away. Yet, he didn't want me and had made a nest with Gina for better or for worse by this stage. He was leaving me emotionally marooned with no means of escape.' Sadly, for Jackie, the pressure did get too much for Keith and he called it a day. 'I never had a chance to thank him and I so desperately want to express gratitude to that man for the fact that he even took a chance with me,' she says poignantly.

Meanwhile, Johnny kept up his occupation as telecommunications connoisseur and was on the phone to Jackie approximately six hours a day (or night). 'By this time I was through the mental breakdown, had attacked Gina in the street, lost a new boyfriend, dropped over three stone in weight, moved house a few times, and changed telephone numbers endlessly. Nothing I did made any difference,' she admits. 'He would still not let go. I developed a cool worrying type of calm. It was almost like a kidnapped woman who stops being scared and decides instead to stare her captor out of it until he breaks. I had a friend in the mid-Shankill who was very good to me at this time. He was, in fact, a saviour. He would keep me on the phone for hours, calming me down, even if it was very late into the night. He would hear the beep beep beeping of the call waiting telling us that Johnny was trying to get through. "I would have never believed it, Jackie, had I not seen it first hand," he told her. This man went and had words with people connected to Johnny, but the constant harassment continued unabated.'

It became apparent that the longer Johnny Adair stayed in prison—through 1996, 1997 and 1998—the more he huffed and puffed and the more he foamed at the mouth. He was in effect showing all the signs of an actual 'mad dog'. For dogs to effectively co-exist with people, they have to be taught that aggressive behaviour will not be tolerated. Instead, that aggression that is innate in dogs has to be channelled into a socially approved form of competitive aggression. In prison, Johnny lacked the competitiveness he needed to survive, but he also lacked the mettle to take out his aggression on his fellow inmates. He needed to find 'vents' elsewhere. 'He hadn't the brains to be political or the balls to be a killer', a close colleague once remarked, although no one can argue that at all times he carried huge sway out on the streets. In the meantime, confined and essentially abandoned,

Mad Dog could only get madder. Signs of a 'sick dog' include: constant whining, barking, howling, poor attention span, snarling and baring the teeth—basically, out and out tense or hyper behaviour. Is there any hope of a cure? Apparently the only short-term solution is to 'back off in distance, duration or intensity with regard to whatever stimulus is provoking your dog'. This is precisely what Jackie was trying to do.

'Some days he was in good form,' Jackie concedes, 'laughing and joking away and reminiscing about our sex life with a load of lads hanging off the end of the receiver listening; Johnny loved an audience. But half an hour later he would be ringing me up again with that "little boy" voice looking for verbal cuddles. He would always manage to talk me around. But just as I felt comfortable enough with him again, he would tell Gina some shit and then it was her turn to phone with her idle threats. As time went on and the years passed, I got more and more aggressive with her. She rang Johnny one time and told him I was psycho, so he rang me and said he was going to get me shot. He often threatened me with a bullet for being "cheeky", but I knew in my heart of hearts that he'd never harm me. He trusted me. On this occasion I begged him to go ahead. I offered to stand out in the front garden and wait for the gunman, or even better, if Gina had the balls to come along herself and do it. No one came.'

The summer months of 1998 were plagued by strife and conflict on the loyalist interface of Belfast. Further afield there was systematic violence across several counties, businesses were attacked, roads were blocked, houses ransacked, and punishment beatings handed out liberally. Statistics later published by the RUC from that year revealed that between 4 and 10 July there had been 1,867 public order offences across Northern Ireland. There had also been 550 attacks on the security forces, 15 shootings and 33 blast bomb attacks carried out by loyalists, 53 RUC officers had been injured, 548 petrol bombs had been thrown, 1,910 petrol bombs recovered, 103 houses and 133 other buildings damaged, 136 cars hijacked, 367 other vehicles damaged, 151 people arrested and 216 plastic bullets fired.

On the most important day of the loyalist calendar, 12 July, the most grotesque and appalling crime of all occurred. Three young Catholic boys, Richard (11), Mark (10) and Jason Ouinn (9), were burnt to death after their home in Ballymoney, Co. Antrim, had been petrol bombed (by the UVF). Communities from both sides were sickened by the attack. 'It is moments like these where innocent victims lose their lives that make everyone stop and think, what are we doing? says Jackie. 'When innocent adults die, they try to make out [on both sides] that it was faulty intelligence or they were sure he/she was involved in this or that, but there was no excusing what happened to those three wee lads. I think that had more of an impact than any politics did at the time.'

Another 'shocker' that year was, of course, the Omagh bomb that killed 29 people when it exploded at 3.10 p.m. in Omagh's High Street. The Real IRA (RIRA), opposed to the Good Friday Agreement, planted the bomb and gave false information regarding its whereabouts to the authorities, encouraging people towards the blast rather than giving them a chance to get away. The death toll represented the single worst incident in Northern Ireland since the beginning of the conflict. Hundreds were injured. It went on to cause further powerful splits within the republican movement. 'Strangely, Johnny never ever mentioned Omagh to me once,' ponders Jackie. 'After being so appalled by the Shankill bomb, he had nothing to say. He tended to harp on more about individuals, this man or that man that was killed. I would scream at him that he was only loyal to dead people. I saw it so many times; people he totally hated when alive became heroes after they had been "taken out". I hate that type of senseless sentiment.'

A year later, on 14 September 1999, the same day that freak hurricanes hit the other side of the Atlantic causing havoc and destruction—Disney World closed down in Florida for the first time in its 28-year history—Johnny Adair breezed out of jail. He sported designer clothes and a designer grin. Crowds of supporters waited to welcome him home to the Shankill. He was the 293rd prisoner to be freed under the Belfast Agreement's early release scheme, having served just over four of his 16-year sentence. He was clearly a happy chappy. Two sizeable UDA flags decorated the turnstile gates of the Maze Prison. Adair flung his fist in the air saluting his supporters.

John White was there to greet him as chairman of the UDP, the political wing of the UFF; he was keen to promote a good image on Adair's behalf. He told reporters that he was there to thank Adair for his unwavering support and decisive role in the peace process. Keen to see Adair off on a good footing, he remarked that Johnny would not be working with Prisoners' Aid to help redevelop the Oldpark area of north Belfast on the peace line between nationalist and loyalist areas. It lasted all of two minutes before Adair was hustled into the back of a car and handed a bullet-proof jacket. He spent the next few days partying wildly, touring his kingdom and playing the philanthropist. He had reams of backing from the ordinary man on the street, but behind the scenes some UDA chiefs were worried he might be too eager to return to bloodshed and ruin the organisation's chances of making political headway on the decommissioning issue.

'He had enemies by the time he left jail. That's now apparent,' says Jackie. 'He managed to piss a lot of people off by shooting his mouth off, so that no one knew where they stood with him because he was so changeable. Real loyalty comes from the heart, but if you haven't got a heart how can you be loyal?' she says. 'I knew it wouldn't be long before he would get himself into trouble again. While I was delighted he was out—don't forget he was married to Gina at the time and under strict instructions from her not to see me "under any circumstances"—I still cared about him a lot and wanted things to work out for him. I kept thinking that there was so much more to him, that if he would only change his ways he could really achieve a lot in life. People will laugh when I say this, but he did have a lot of gifts. He was extremely influential and thought long and hard about things. He had a huge impact on Northern Ireland for a young kid who grew up in a poor area and left school with not much real hope of a future.'

However, Jackie's memory of that time doesn't revolve around the day he got out of jail for good, but six months before, on 21 March, when Jay Adair was born. 'He was let out for the birth,' she explains. 'He made a point of phoning me to tell me of the happy event. I was totally cut up inside as I had wanted a child with him so much. For any woman to be put in that position, it's excruciating. It attacks your most basic instincts that the man you love, and who tells you that he loves you, decides to have a child with the woman he constantly gives out about. I was sick. I was just about to have a bath when Johnny ran up the stairs and rushed towards me; I hadn't heard him come into the house at all. I was standing there stark naked when he said to me, "What the fuck are you doing?", I was doing the washing, so I said to him, "What the fuck does it look like I'm doing?" He began telling me how beautiful the baby was, his wee hands and what not. My stomach was churning; nothing could take the hurt away from me. I took him into the bedroom and sent him on home with a big smile on his face. It certainly wasn't a triumph of any sort, but it did make me feel better for an hour or two, knowing that he came straight from the hospital around to my place.'

Not long after, again when he was out on parole on 30 April, his favourite band UB40 were playing and Johnny said he wouldn't miss it for the world. 'I advised him not to go to the concert,' says Jackie. 'Where it was taking place, the area it was in, good God it didn't take a moment's consideration to figure it out. I told him to make sure to bring people with him for security, but Gina had said that it was "their" country and they should be able to go where they wanted. This is after the deaths of dozens of people for which he was thought to be responsible, and he's out parading around the streets! Of course, he was recognised. I was at the concert myself with my daughter. On the way out she spotted a pool of blood, but I told her it was tomato sauce. Johnny had been shot in the head. I knew it was a "damp round" the minute I heard he had been shot. I know a bit about guns. Adair was lucky to escape with his life (seven out of nine lives gone by this stage). Not only did he take the "damp round" but a crowd also turned on him and Gina and began beating them after he was shot. Bystanders said they saw Adair being beaten by around 12 men. While the RUC treated the attack as "attempted murder", no one was ever identified formally as having carried it out. He was back in jail, after being out on parole, recovering, and

I went in to see him. "Do you know what you could do for me, Jack," he said. "Write away there to UB40 and tell them your boyfriend was shot at their concert and could you get him their autographs." That's all he cared about, not that the IRA or whoever else wanted him dead.

'I rang him a few days later on the Monday and said to him, "Johnny, has Gina got you insured yet?" to which he replied, "Don't be so stupid!" On the Wednesday he phoned again. "Why did you ask me if Gina got me insured?" She had gone out and done just that, telling him that she had to make sure the kids would be provided for if anything happened to him. Can you imagine what the premiums were like? I asked him how much, but he simply said he wasn't sure. She just got him to sign.

'Johnny was back on the road again, drinking and acting the lad,' Jackie smiles. 'I started seeing him again now and then. Well, it was actually impossible to avoid him, and even if I did, he'd just call around anyway. We had been out at the Shankill shebeen and were making our way home in a taxi. His friend Dick Dempsey was sitting in the back and he was winding me up saying that he had been "bucking Johnny" for a good few years and that only the two of them knew about it. It was all said in fun, but something about the intonation in his voice turned my gut. He was staring at Johnny, looking for his reaction, and Johnny's laugh was a bit strained in return. It was like they were making a joke of the truth. It was well known that Dick was bisexual. He went with women but he preferred men, or boys as he put it. I looked at Johnny and asked him straight out if it was true. "And what would you think of it if it was, Jackie?" I said I couldn't care less what he was into, but he might let me know if he was sticking his cock in men's arses because he was also sleeping with me and I didn't want to catch anything. It was still a joke at this stage. But then I asked him if Gina knew, and he just nodded a "no". There was something striking in the silence of that gesture; it wasn't so much a joke then, and I knew it was real. "You're not Gina; I trust you," he said. I blanked it. I didn't want to believe it. But deep down I knew it was true. I certainly knew they weren't joking. You could cut the atmosphere with a knife in the car and I was certain that they'd been humping one another. I think quite possibly he may have tried it when he was younger, and there may have been one or two incidents in his adult life. I guess if you try something like that, then it becomes open to you, doesn't it? On top of this, there were a great many rumours about his sexuality. Where did they spring from? Were they all unsubstantiated? One thing is for sure, he'd often ask me for anal sex and it was something I didn't fancy at all. It can't be that hygienic, can it? He'd get really turned on by it though, but then again so are a lot of men.'

Michael Stone has since alleged that in prison Johnny confessed to him that he was bisexual, adding that he participated in a threesome involving 'man on man and man on woman'. If that sounds complicated, his auxiliary sexual fantasies were much more middle-of-the-road and misaligned with his staunch, stout-hearted image. Jackie said his favourite sexual fantasy was to pretend he was a 16-year-old virgin being propositioned by an older woman on his way home from school. 'I would tell him I was going to spank him very hard and then show him a few things that he'd need to know about the big bad world when he got out there after his schooldays were over,' she jibes. 'His eyes would light up and he'd say, "Please don't hurt me Mrs. I have to get home to my Ma for my tea", and it would truly turn him on.

'At this time Johnny and Gina had moved up to Manor Street, right beside the peace line and she dyed her hair black to give herself a new start. She probably thought the new hairstyle came with a new reputation, for now that Johnny was home she would have to behave. I found it strange where they were living as all the Provos had to do was fire a rocket over the fence and they would have toasted them completely.

'On Christmas Day that year he came into my home with a friend of his, and Johnny and I went upstairs for a bit of time alone. At some point the friend burst open the door and began taking photographs of us having sex. I jumped up and got a bit upset, but the two of them just laughed. I said to him, "You better destroy them." In good faith I thought that he would. At the end of January 2000, he rang one day and said. "Meet me at the bottom of the street. We're going for a drive." We went to a house in Tiger's Bay where I knew some of the "good time" girls hung out. Johnny was sitting back enjoying the banter. I got up to get a glass of water in the kitchen and I could hear them all laughing. My stomach sank. I knew in my heart of hearts he was showing them the photographs. I came back into the room and some of the prostitutes looked highly amused. "Give me the photos," I screamed at him, but he just continued laughing. "Relax. I'll destroy them," he said, but he didn't give a shit and these women thought it was hilarious. He knew I was really upset. When we got into the car, he was in the back seat between me and this prostitute. He kept up the gas all the way home. "You don't mind if she sucks me off, do you, Jack?" I couldn't believe what I was hearing. When I got home I roared crying. He rang me about an hour later and said, "For fuck's sake, Jackie, they're only a couple of whores. There's no harm in them at all."

'A few weeks later he rang me one day and said, "We're down here at Dublin Street handing out cards to prostitutes." He asked if he and Ian Truesdale could call around, so I said OK. This girl came in with him and she had the maddest pair of knockers I've ever seen in my life, totally huge; she had had about three operations. "Not bad those buns, eh?" Johnny said, pointing at her tits. I could barely take my eyes off them. They looked totally unnatural. She'd had her cheeks done too, and her stomach. I asked her where she got the money for all this and I could see this guy who was with her looking me up and down. I had a pair of shorts on and a wee top because that's the way I ran about the house. Johnny asked me to get him photographs of us, but I didn't want to move. They weren't "those" photographs, I may add here; they were ordinary ones I had of Johnny that were taken for a book. When I sat down, Johnny said to the guy, "What do you think of her, mate? She's got a good shape for her age, hasn't she?" I didn't know if that was a compliment or not. "Can I ask you something?" Truesdale said. "How would you like to earn £800 a week?" Well, my heart just sank. I knew what he was proposing but I just didn't want to believe it. "Are you asking me what I think you're asking me?" He looked at Johnny and then back at me and said, "Look, you don't have to go the whole way.

A lot of these men just want a wank or a blow job?" He started listing off a lot of names, people that I knew I'd be working with, and I have to say some of the names surprised me. Some were the women of well-known figureheads and what have you. I kept calm, looked at Johnny and decided to test him. "Well Johnny, what do you say?" I asked him. He shrugged his shoulders and replied, "You're young, free and single. It's nothing to do with me." I lifted my fist and planted one right in the middle of his ugly face and broke his nose there and then.

"'You are one evil bastard!" I yelled, the tears streaming down my face. He was hopping mad, and with blood streaming down his face shouting back at me, "How the fuck am I going to explain this to Gina?" He threatened me and told me to shut my mouth and all sorts of things. "Get out of my fucking house," I ordered. I turned to Truesdale and advised him. "Why don't you go down and ask Johnny's wife. She gives it away for free." I went to the housing people the next day and put in for a new house, telling them that I was being intimidated. I moved five weeks later and didn't look back. Johnny had a saying that we were like two magnets that would always be drawn back to each other. But you know what? He was wrong. I never saw him again.'

07 | NOT A HOLLYWOOD ENDING

There's been talk doing the rounds of a bounty on Johnny's head, but I maintain he'll still try and return home regardless. He might think that he can live in peace and harmony for the rest of his days, but there's more chance of a united Ireland than that happening. He has sealed his own fate and it doesn't matter how long he's away, nothing can change the facts now.

Today, Jackie shares her flat in east Belfast with a paramilitary budgie called Bubbles, who though probably wholly unaware, served a five-year sentence at Maghaberry Prison. It was there as a baby that he learnt how to speak true loyalist invective. Although his vocabulary is limited, there can be no doubt as to which side of the fence his politics rest. 'Up the Shankill!', 'Rangers', 'Go on ye bastards', 'Give us a cup of tea' and an endearing wolf whistle when a lady walks into the room are just a few of his enthusiastic offerings to 'the cause'. At the same time he doesn't seem to understand that the war is over and there's no real need to take sides any more. The fact that he lived in a cage within a cage convinced Jackie that he should live a life of undeterred freedom in post-ceasefire Northern Ireland. He now has the full run of her flat and flies about at great speed. Despite the fact that he squawks and fights with flying feathers to get out of his cage, when out, he often changes his mind and chooses to institutionalise himself by soaring back inside. 'He'd remind you a bit of Johnny,' Jackie jokes. 'He's having a wee bit of trouble trying to negotiate his freedom.'

She may have a point. Johnny, living a tranquil life on social welfare benefits in the middle-class seaside town of Troon, Ayrshire, is having a bit of trouble negotiating his freedom too. He is barred from *all* the pubs in the town; no reason is given apart from posters with his mug-shot and the dubious instruction, 'Do Not Serve This Man'. Still, he's happy for the time being scoffing burgers with brown sauce in high-class hotel lobbies amidst 'ladies who lunch' and golfing marvels, but his heart remains across the water in Ulster. The rest of the story is the stuff that makes Hollywood blink and then blink again just to make sure the producer got it right and wasn't doing too much 'coke'. Terror chief gets out of jail and is pursued by not only erstwhile enemies, but by a crazed UK lotto winner who wants to fling all his cash at him, an indulgent football hooligan who wants Adair to give seminars alongside him, and a bunch of German skinheads who have set up a German C Company in his honour. Furthermore, in the night clubs and band halls of Glasgow and beyond, revellers run to shake his hand and seek an autograph, while women continue to beseech him into bed. He is equally taunted as a luminous star as he is haunted by death threats, which is making the end of the Adair 'life production' disastrously indecisive. He could easily come to at least a dozen different ends or, most surprising of all, no particular end at all. Will the UVF kill him? Will it be an old adversary intent on personal justice? Or will he return home and become a dyed-in-the-wool politician or take a job as a postman in some far-off country where no one knows him? Another irony is that his surname in Gaelic means 'noble, exalted, leader, strong as an oak'. Yet, in another ordinary Protestant life in another city, his fate would have simply been unemployed, untutored thug in a baseball cap who eats steroids for breakfast. 'They [the UDA] won't come and get me,' he recently stated. 'Sure they couldn't even get halfway across the peace line to shoot me way back then when I lived in Belfast, so I reckon they won't come to Scotland.'

He was supposed to be dead before Christmas 2002 and still refuses to wear a bullet-proof vest, so obviously the protagonist in the tale is just as unsure of his own outcome as the audience.

For now, he spends only short spells in Troon itself. Instead he regularly holes up in Glasgow, Huddersfield and Bolton to evade assassination. It doesn't stop the locals from being excusably wary. Here he sits in wait for the UDA to implode before he can realise his dream of returning to the Shankill and repossessing his loyalist throne. While Jackie's prophecy of a final split from Gina happened in October 2005, it has been since rumoured that he has taken a Troon mistress who is only hazily aware of his disreputable past. He was also hunted down by the UK tabloid media in July 2006 outside a not-so-glamorous two-star hotel in Turkey arm in arm with a 20-something-year-old blonde. Ironically, her name is also Jacqueline, his latest sexual dupe. Remarkably the youthful woman is younger than his eldest daughter and was very taken with the émigré terror boss. Manchester police allegedly 'hounded him' out of his previous home, and now Strathclyde police are on constant alert. As a UK citizen he is not constrained as to where he lives and socialises, but put one foot wrong and he could easily find himself in a situation similar to Bubbles. Except this time Jackie won't be opening and closing the cage.

'Knowing Johnny as I do, I estimate that he sits and obsesses about coming home, plotting, planning, meditating on it constantly,' she says. 'He'll be saying to himself, I've plenty of support back there; it's just that they can't come out and say it at the moment because "them uns" [current UDA leadership] have all my people on the ground brainwashed. If I sit and wait it will all come good. He'll talk endlessly about the war being over, and he might imagine that he'll just come home and get a job and live peacefully or get involved in the public relations side of politics, but deep down he'll be thinking, they need me there in case the whole situation goes tits up in Northern Ireland again. You can't trust the IRA even if they have thrown away their guns. It'll be 150 per cent me, myself and I. The only reason he's in Scotland is because he's got a bit of support there and he feels safe. He won't believe for a minute that they'll come and get him. And, to be honest, I hope they don't, because life simply would not be interesting without waiting to see what Johnny Adair will do next. I mean, look at all that nonsense going on at the moment with the new C Company in Dresden!'

Adair has attracted the attention and admiration of a group of young German skinheads who have taken the extraordinary step of casing their bodies in C Company and UFF tattoos. The terror appendage has set up a type of 'away squad' of C Company in his honour in the domicile of fine porcelain china, Dresden. The chief figurehead, Nick, took it a step further by getting a huge slogan, 'Simply the Best', splattered across his back and is convinced Johnny is a political figurehead like no other. He sees Adair as being a redeemer for Northern Ireland, a combatant who took up a war on behalf of loyalist communities under gratuitous attack. It is clear he has a scant idea of the anguish that nationalist communities were put through for decades before the Troubles really detonated in the late 1960s. Chris, second in command of the Dresden outfit, has the UDA's inimitable slogan, '*Quis Separabit*' strewn across his tanned belly. Nick is currently in prison for gun possession, but has vowed to cultivate support for Adair in other German cities sometime soon. A Belfast newspaper recently published a photograph of Adair drinking with his *ergebene Anhänger* (devoted followers) grinning gleefully. Johnny unquestionably stands out from the crowd; for a start he looks about two decades older and is the only one in the crowd who appears world weary, somnolent and bewildered. Nick wrote to Adair before his release from Maghaberry Prison in early 2005, and decided to take up the loyalist cause in the Fatherland. His tumbledown C Company cluster has also personally apologised to Adair for 'what Hitler did', and with that modest matter out of the way, the merger is said to be now complete. The duo plan to do some international travelling together and when Nick is out of the slammer he's going to take Adair to Namibia for a holiday to 'view other races' and broaden their political resolve.

'Johnny will go anywhere he has support, wherever people will look up to him and make him feel big about himself,' asserts Jackie. 'He has always been in denial and he will keep going that way for the rest of his life. There is now no need for the Johnny Adairs of this world to play the role that was previously demanded of them. How ironic is it that in peace Johnny is lost? What actual role could he play in politics in the North of Ireland now? From what I've read in newspaper articles recently, he believes the IRA's decommissioning manoeuvre is genuine, but privately I'd say he doesn't believe a word of it. On one level, as far as he's concerned the IRA is no longer killing Protestant people and the armed struggle is over, even if he hates them. Yet, on another level, that leaves him with no role, nothing to do, no identity. He was there to defend his country from the threat of republican violence. That gave him something to do apart from being a hood living in the Shankill. The UDA are a defence organisation, but if Ulster is no longer being attacked, there is nothing to defend. Instead what he's doing is turning the combat inwards. To him the current UDA are a load of thugs; if they were offered enough money they would decommission. He believes that if the leadership as it stands disbanded, the people on the ground, who up until now have been against him, could be convinced otherwise, that the past could be put to rest and he would be king of the castle once again. It's sad.'

Adair has not lived as a free man in Belfast since 2003, although in early 2006 he tiptoed back to the Shankill with documentary maker and reporter Donal MacIntyre. He sauntered around within yards of enemy homes, knocking on the door of prime foe Jim Spence. 'He couldn't face me. He hadn't the balls to come to the door,' he later commented. 'I hope one day I face them all.' He publicly maintains that he is now fully acquiescent to peace. And while it cannot be denied that C Company was once to the UDA what the SAS was to the British Army, and that throughout the North it was the outfit more feared and most respected, Adair now has little or no trust in the current leadership. He views it as corrupt and ineffectual. 'That organisation is run by a convicted rapist who was shot in both legs by the UDA at one time, and another corrupt bastard,' he told the British journalist. In spite of this, he is still said to be quite shocked at the level of betrayal he received from his devoted faction of foot soldiers.

Jim Spence's disloyalty and betrayal has hurt Adair the most. He was after all instrumental in the night of the long knives against C Company in 2002/03. While others in C Company hated Spence to the extent of wanting him dead, Adair when he was king tolerated, protected and covered for him. Spence was essentially the jester, the clown in Adair's court. He was and is a real comedian, with a nippy turn of phrase and attention-grabbing jabs. Johnny considered him to be clued in and clever and the shock of his betrayal is made all the worse because Adair has never done anything personal against him.

'I can imagine how hurt Johnny is about Spence,' acknowledges Jackie. 'The way he'll handle it will be to pass him off as a tout. Johnny basically has two categories of people in his head: the first is a tout or thug and the second, usually referring to women, is a whore or a woman scorned. He needs to pigeon-hole people to simplify things. Johnny loved Spence because he was smart and had that bit more to him. Spence was one of the guys who tried to talk Johnny around when he cut a deal for the 16-year prison sentence in 1995. He really felt he cared about him. But it's not just Spence; he has a lot of enemies now and that's down to how he treated people.'

Other adversaries whom Adair was able to identify didn't make it out of the feud alive. In February 2003, UDA brigadier John 'Grugg' Gregg, the would-be assassin of Gerry Adams and later Adair's associate, along with UDA member Robert Carson, were shot and killed in Belfast. They were in a taxi that was rammed by their assassins. Although to this day Adair claims he had nothing to do with his murder, it is known that after Grugg had daringly disclosed that there were 'four graves dug out for C Company leaders', Adair took considerable offence. A close nark of Adair's claims that after Grugg's murder, Adair commented: 'He wanted confrontation and he got it, that's for sure. He sat idle for years and years and let the Protestant people get slaughtered all around him. He said he had four graves dug and he had C

Company leaders picked for them, including myself. He sent two monkeys to John White's house and planted a bomb. He was trying to be a big boy. He wanted to take on the Shankill, but where is he now? He's dead and I'm still alive.' Whether he was involved or not, it directly sealed Adair's fate at the time (he was held responsible for ordering the murders), and immediately Gina Adair and around twenty families from the Shankill fled their homes for the UK after being told by the UDA leadership that staying would incur the penalty of death.

More recently, in October 2005, Jim Gray, aged 47, the flashy former leader of the UDA in east Belfast, was shot outside his father's house removing gym equipment from his car on the Clarawood estate. He was out on bail and had been stopped by the police near Banbridge, Co. Down, in an attempt to flee the country with a €10,000 bank draft and £3,000 in cash. Gray had, according to those close to him, struck a deal with the police on his release from jail in return for vital information on unsolved loyalist crimes. The 'Bling Brigadier', as he was sometimes nicknamed, was famed for his ostentatious and even camp dress sense. He ruled east Belfast for years from his Avenue One Bar on the Newtownards Road, and later bought the Bunch of Grapes pub on the Beersbridge Road. Gray had been trying to 'turn a corner' and dissociate himself from paramilitary activities and was supposedly training to be a Christian pastor at the time of his death. 'I couldn't care less about Jim Gray's early demise', Adair remarked after his death. 'This was a man that plotted to kill me and my family; he sent two men to try to kill me when I was dropping my kids off at school.'

The fall from grace for loyalist's self-serving king goes back much further than either of those incidents. He had been freed from prison initially in 1999 under the auspices of the Good Friday Agreement early release scheme, but was soon 'stirring it' on his home territory with drug dealing and extortion, among other activities. Before he was returned to prison for breaching licence conditions in August 2000, huge rifts formed between the UDA and the UVF, resulting in bad blood as well as ferocious blood-letting.

'Johnny was away on holidays (he went to Spain with Gina every year to give her a break from the kids) when Mark Fulton was found dead in prison,' says Jackie. 'He took that real bad and thought he might have been done in at first, but it looked like he had topped himself. He started messing around with boys from the LVF and I knew what was going through his head: I'll get in with this lot here and take them over. I had bumped into Fulton in the Avenue One Bar one night not long before that. We were always good friends. He would come out and have a laugh with us and let his hair down a bit—something he couldn't do around Billy Wright as Wright was very strict with his men and very anti-drug. Anyway, he says to me, "Have you seen the wee fella lately?" I told him that I no longer took up with Johnny. Then he went on to tell me he had been up to the prison to see him. The minute I heard that, I knew Johnny was trying to take over the LVF.'

On 21 July, the UFF shot dead Gerard Lawlor, a 19-year-old Catholic (chosen randomly) following the murder of a 19-year-old Protestant earlier that week. Lawlor's murder was a type of favour from C Company to the LVF, apparently on Johnny's instructions. A fragmentary feud between the LVF and the UVF dragged on throughout the year. Martin Taylor (35), a member of the UVF, was shot dead while working on a wall outside a house in Ballysillan, Belfast. The LVF was believed to be responsible for his killing. In January 2000, Richard Jameson (46), a member of the UVF, was shot dead outside his home near Portadown, Co. Armagh. The LVF claimed responsibility. In May they also killed another UVF man, Martin Taylor (35). So for Johnny to be seen to support the LVF, although clandestinely, meant coming out against the UVF. While there was trouble at Drumcree in July, the politicians were nevertheless still trundling towards an out and out peace agreement. Seventy-six paramilitary prisoners were released from the Maze under the Good Friday Agreement early release scheme and British troops were also reduced to a level unseen since the 1970s.

'It was very up and down the entire time,' says Jackie. 'In one respect there was this movement towards peace, but the streets were getting crazier by the week. There was a definite turning point after the August loyalist show of strength when Johnny and Michael Stone stood on a platform together and Gina waved an AK-47 around the place wearing a short skirt. Afterwards they marched up the Shankill and there were some words exchanged between Johnny and some UVF blokes outside a bar. By the time August came round there was full-scale warfare between the different loyalist groups. These were the same people who used to party with us seven or eight years before.'

After the 'show of strength', a gun attack took place on the Rex Bar following a confrontation between the UVF and the UFF/LVF. The bar was thronged with a crowd of up to 300 loyalists and shots were fired after attempts to enter the bar failed (it was a UVF hangout). Johnny had led the march with a group of men carrying UDA/UFF flags, but there was also a young bloke carrying an LVF flag.

'Even if within that march someone is carrying a tricolour, it's none of the UVF's business,' Johnny remarked afterwards. 'What gave the UVF the right to go over and stick a glass into the wee band man's face and tell him to take the flag down? There are channels that you go through to resolve these issues and they were not used. At the end of the day it was a loyalist flag.'

Houses were ransacked that night; in excess of 14 houses were plundered in the Lower Shankill area, with some being set alight. Shots could be heard all over the Shankill but according to Jackie, this was predicted well in advance by Adair and his colleagues.

'He deliberately had that guy with the LVF flag at the Rex Bar to spark the feuding,' she maintains. 'Weapons had already been brought into the Shankill by Gina and another woman before the feud, and weapons were also stashed in UDA headquarters, so it was all planned or at least if it wasn't planned it was foretold by some manner or means. It ripped the community apart. It didn't have to kick off the way it did. That's what everyone felt, that it was totally unnecessary; but everywhere Johnny Adair treads there is always disturbance.'

On 21 August Jackie Coulter (a companion of Johnny Adair) and Bobby Mahood were killed by the UVF. Counter-attacks were carried out on offices used by the two loyalist parties closely associated with the UDA and the UVF as well as more retaliatory murders. A house next door to Billy Hutchinson of the Progressive Unionist Party (PUP), the UVF's political wing, was peppered with bullets. A revenge attack befell 21-year-old Samuel Rocket, a UVF member, at his Oldpark home where he was shot in front of his girlfriend and their one-year-old daughter. The UFF said it carried out the attack as a reprisal for the double killing just days before. Troops were deployed on the streets of Belfast to control the situation that didn't look likely to end any day soon. The two loyalist factions lived cheek by jowl on the Shankill Road, so tensions were heightening. 'There was this terrible feeling of anger about the place,' says Jackie. 'This was loyalists fighting loyalists and I dunno, but maybe unfairly Johnny was getting blamed on a lot, but it had taken on a power of its own. You have to remember, by that time the Shankill Road had suffered more than 25 years of violence, but that was usually caused by republicans. That road suffered more than anywhere else in the entire Troubles in terms of people murdered and houses and businesses destroyed. Every time there's a feud like the one in 2000, dozens of families have to get out as well.'

The day before Rocket's murder, Johnny was arrested and returned to prison by the order of Peter Mandelson, then Secretary of State for Northern Ireland. The arrest was an attempt to suppress the feud and the likelihood of further killings, but it didn't really do much good. Traditionally loyalists had no means of mediation to resolve intense feuds, unlike republicans who in the past had often used Clonard Monastery in west Belfast for intercession. By December 2000, with Adair back behind bars, a total of seven people had lost their lives before an operative compromise was reached. Adair was adamant that he would be released from prison, but as part of the licence stipulation it meant a prisoner should not support an organisation that was not on ceasefire (the UFF was not listed as a recognised organisation) and prisoners were also prohibited from the commission, preparation or instigation of acts of terrorism or be a danger to the public. Johnny had failed on two counts, so Mandelson's plan to keep him cell-bound was met.

'I was no longer in touch with him, but I had said a dozen times over that he would be booted back inside jail after the feuds,' says Jackie. 'Sure, even that October there was an attempt on Jonty Brown's life and everyone knew that was bound to be Johnny's doing. He hated Brown. So even from inside jail once again he was getting some "work" done.'

A year later, on 15 May 2002, Adair was released having reached the halfway point of his original sentence. With the help of comrade John White, Adair set about reinventing himself as a serious thinker. He took a 'real job' as a prisoners' welfare co-ordinator (publicly funded) and engaged in various political exertions including meeting up with Northern Ireland Secretary John Reid. After he was released, he was honoured with a plaque from the LVF that bore the inscription 'Brothers in Arms'. Even though a large gathering of UDA and UVF men were there to meet him outside the gates of Maghaberry Prison, there could no longer be any doubts as to Adair's affiliation with the LVF. Slowly and surely he began falling out with the UDA leadership and friends such as Jackie McDonald, John Gregg, Andre Shoukri, Billy McFarland and Jim Gray.

'He started stirring the shit again, didn't he?' remarks Jackie. 'When Stephen Warnock was killed in September [he was LVF], Johnny was told not to go to his funeral but went anyhow. That was a horrible incident because his wee daughter who was only 3 years old was in the car with him and saw the whole thing. The word was that he owed £10,000 drugs money. There was also talk doing the rounds that Jim Gray had something to do with his death, but I don't think they ever got to prove that. Anyhow, that's what Johnny thought.'

According to Adair, a member of the east Belfast UDA approached the Inner Council and said that he was a witness to Jim Gray and another man killing Stephen Warnock. It later emerged that this man was making it up. However, Jim Gray was given the opportunity to come before the Inner Council and explain himself but declined, which in the eyes of many was an admission of guilt.

Jim Gray was himself shot (but survived after stumbling to the nearby Garnerville Police Training College, where he received emergency treatment) when he tried to pay his respects to the Warnock family. Another UDA man who was with Gray at the time was also shot, but again he survived. Adair was blamed for the shooting but is adamant that he had nothing to do with it, that it was the work of the LVF. When Adair along with John White and Andre Shoukri decided to attend Warnock's funeral, the UDA were appalled. To them it was the zenith of disloyalty to attend a funeral where the 'shooter', who had attempted to take Jim Gray and his colleague's life, would be in attendance. Johnny Adair later stated his reason for attending the funeral: 'If you're my friend and you're killed, I will go to your funeral regardless if it's the UVF or the UDA who say "stay away". My friendship with that person comes first.'

After the funeral, Adair was sent for to account for his actions. 'He would have considered himself way beyond the UDA leadership by this stage,' explains Jackie. 'He thought they were a bunch of "jinnys" that had sat on their arses while he fought the war, so he would not have liked it at all that he had to explain himself to these people'.

UDA men and the police lined the streets expecting altercations. Adair was accompanied by Fat Jackie Thompson (who would later attempt to kill him in Bolton in 2005) and Sham Millar. The leaders of five of the six UDA command areas—north, south and east Belfast, south-east Antrim and north Antrim/Derry—determined that Adair had put the overall organisation in an impossible situation and that he was no longer recognised as a UDA member. Adair left and went straight to an LVF meeting point where he told his new-found cronies of the meeting, and in so doing, his fate was sealed.

The next day the UDA issued a statement: 'The officers and men of the UDA right across Northern Ireland due to recent events re-state that none of its members played any role or part in the death of Stephen Warnock. It has since come to light that certain people have been acting as *agents provocateurs* between the Ulster Defence Association and the Loyalist Volunteer Force to capitalise on events for their own recent purposes. As a result of ongoing investigations the present brigadier of west Belfast is no longer acceptable in our organisation.'

They also threw out John White, even though he was officially a member of the Ulster Political Research Group (UPRG) and not the UDA. There was thought to be a lot of jealousy surrounding John White at the time from men like Jackie McDonald as well as resentment towards Adair's backing of White.

'Johnny got thrown out for being a stupid bastard, surprise, surprise!' says Jackie. 'As far as Johnny is concerned, he had no part in the feud that followed because he wasn't directly confronted by these men who opposed him.'

An intense campaign of anti-Adair propaganda started to rear its head in loyalist publications such as the *Warrior*. In one sarcastic leaflet left around bars on the Shankill Road, Johnny was described as 'Johnny Adolf Adair', who 'tells the cops everything'. It goes on: 'Adair unfortunately has been temporarily removed by his handlers . . . we the loyalist people of the Shankill Road would have preferred a more permanent removal.'

'It became increasingly anti-Adair in autumn that year,' says Jackie. 'There were all these skits about the UDA standing for Ulster Detests Adair and other such stuff. It was clear he was losing his status and this time it was going to get pulled from under his arse for good'.

The feud persisted all the way through autumn and winter. On 4 October LVF member Geoffrey Grey was shot dead as he left a pub on Ravenhill Avenue in east Belfast. Grey, a father of four, previously lived in Portadown but had lived on the Beersbridge Road in south-east Belfast for just over a year. Residents tried to administer first aid but he died at the scene. He had been an associate of the murdered LVF leader Billy Wright and was a member of the guard of honour at his funeral, connections which made him a target for rival loyalist paramilitaries. In retaliation, the LVF shot 22-year-old Alex McKinley three days afterwards; he died of gunshot wounds on 13 October. Five days later the LVF issued a statement declaring the right to protect its members from attack. This proclamation was interpreted by loyalist mediators as offering a no first-strike policy, whereby there would be no attacks on the UDA if the LVF in turn was not attacked. Intelligence passed to the feuding organisation alleged that Jim Gray had nothing to do with Warnock's murder. It seems Johnny had over-reacted once again.

'It didn't end there,' says Jackie. 'How could it? They may have said it's all OK now, you can return home and live happily ever after, but these men just don't let things go. When lives are lost, your enemies cannot be forgotten.'

At the beginning of November, a spokesman for the UPRG was shot in both legs in the Ballysillan area of north Belfast. A statement issued by the UDA claimed he had been brought before paramilitary chiefs following a four-month investigation. 'Johnny began to lose it completely and turned on his lifelong friends at this stage. That's how I knew he was painting himself out of the picture,' claims Jackie. 'Winkie Dodds, for instance, his lifelong friend, would have taken a bullet in the head for him at any stage, and he turned against him. He had accused Winkie's wife's brother of being a tout and the guy had to move from Belfast. It was the ultimate betrayal in my eyes and the point of his undeniable downfall. Then Winkie and his wife were put out of their estate (they moved up to Whitewell). Poor Winkie has had terrible health problems since that have been well documented. He's not a well man and I'm sure he must be kicking himself today that he supported Johnny for so long. Then Spence was next, and Alan McClean, his welfare officer, basically all his closest friends. Even though he had broken my heart only two years before, I was glad I wasn't still seeing him; it would have put my life and the life of my kids in grave danger.'

An attempt was made on Adair's life in December as he dropped his kids off to school—he attributed this to Jim Gray—and Christmas didn't pass without violence either. On 27 December, a young man aged 22, Jonathan Stewart, was shot dead at a get-together simply because he was a nephew of Alan McClean who had been expelled from the Shankill a few months earlier. Roy Green, a previous military commander with the UDA, was also killed in revenge. By January the authorities had had enough and decided to pluck Adair off the streets once more.

This time he would complete his full sentence and would not be released until 2005. A month later John Gregg was murdered, and from this point onwards Adair's supporters and family members were ordered to leave the Shankill under the threat of death. Dozens of families were condemned to compulsory exile. Fat Jackie Thompson, Sham Millar, Wayne Dowie (who would later become Gina's live-in lover and the reason why Adair would beat her up so viciously on his release from a UK prison in 2005), Ian Truesdale, John White, Gina Adair (and children), Gina's mother, and at least a dozen other families left Ireland for good. At first they tried to settle in Ayr, but later moved down towards Manchester and Bolton, where the majority still live today.

A flurry of antagonistic anti-Adair natter in loyalist publications has since alluded to the fact that Adair and White's support for peace was only a ruse that would lead them to further personal gains. An editorial from the *Warrior* loyalist news-sheet at the time read: 'Both these men for years now have acted as *agents provocateurs* in order to bring about the destruction of the UDA. There is now a consensus of opinion within most of the leadership of that organisation that one or both of these men have been in the pocket of the Northern Ireland Office for several years.' Both men were effectively blamed for the sinking reputation of the UDA from a serious political organisation into a plethora of drug dealing and 'other detestable' activities. 'Both men have been involved in the sale of illegal drugs yet they've never been charged for these offences', the *Warrior* claimed. 'When we see the corruption on the scale that these two men are responsible for, never again let us allow this once proud organisation to be trailed through the gutter for the sake of personal advancement. To Adair and White we say what your mate Gerry Adams would say, *Slán Abhaile*—time to go—may you both rot and burn in hell.'

Strong words and even stronger sentiment, but these days it's not the UDA that Johnny is wary of; it's the UVF. 'Johnny considers the UVF to be more intelligent, professional and dangerous,' says Jackie. 'According to him, the UDA is just a bunch of criminal thugs with no intelligence, who can make drugs and sell drugs, but they don't know how to put a good military operation together.'

Adair himself feels that the UDA brigade staff of west Belfast is solely to blame for the last inexorable feud that has sealed the fate of his family and friends for good. 'I would love to come face to face and confront them,' he told a British journalist in early 2006. 'I believe that the mindset in these so-called leaders of loyalists is crooked and when they are removed, it will be safe for me to return,' he said. 'I feel hatred for what they've done to my friends and family, for how our lives have been turned upside down. I have lots of support but because I'm not "there" these people are able to poison and brainwash and intimidate my followers.'

It's obvious that his heart is as embedded in the Shankill as the colourful murals that continue to grace its parapets. However, Johnny would hardly be impressed with the modern-day murals in his name—a lot of these are no longer in existence— which appeared in the run-up to his release from prison in January 2005 and continued to the end of that year: 'Your Days are Numbered Pimp Adair' (January 2005), 'Bring it On. Fuck J. Adair' (January 2005), 'J. Adair Prod Killer' (January 2005), 'C U Soon Fuck U. J. Adair C/Coy' (October 2004), 'Adair Loyalist Wife Beater' (November 2005). These murals were painted around the same locations where three and four years previously entirely converse sentiments declared: 'His Only Crime is Loyalty' (2001), 'Free Johnny Adair' (2001). With ordinary people being unable to vent their anger at the havoc let loose on the Shankill, the walls did all their talking.

What Gina Adair must have been thinking when she caught the ferry from Belfast to Cairnryan on 5 February 2003 is anyone's guess, but one thing was certain, she would never again rule the roost in her elite enclave of the Lower Shankill. She has been told in no uncertain terms that returning home will be answered by certain death. As the banished crew stepped off the boat to an uncertain future, Dumfries and Galloway police were on hand to question them and analyse their every move. Likewise, in Manchester and Bolton, where the bulk of the exiles settled, the police have not left them alone. But the main bugbear has been the UK media who have not only demonised them with their own special blend of tabloid vile, but they have consistently let their enemies back home know of their whereabouts.

'It was like watching balls in a pin ball machine and trying to predict where they'd smash into next,' says Jackie. 'It was compulsive reading, like those cheap celebrity magazines. I mean, I heard within a very short time that Gina was back to her old tricks and was seeing a man 15 years younger than her. It was straight back to the old ways. Neither of them will change their ways; that's why they made the perfect couple.'

By April 2003 a roving squad of UFF foot soldiers, once staunchly devoted to Adair, were carrying out attacks against the 'Bolton Wanderers'. Gunmen discharged several rounds of ammunition outside Gina Adair's house in Bolton and she was forced to flee with her kids. Stories appeared in local newspapers about property devaluing on the street. Adair at this stage was still whiling away his time in prison. Analogous of biblical language about lepers, the UFF issued a statement explaining their reasoning for attacking the 'outcasts'. The UFF said: 'As a result of an ongoing investigation into the murder of John Gregg, Robert Carson and other criminal activities by Adair and his associates, last night an ASU [active service unit] of the Ulster Freedom Fighters attempted to oust members of the Adair faction in Bolton, England. As the investigation continues and more evidence is uncovered, action will be taken against anyone providing guns or a safe haven for these outcasts. They will be moved on wherever they are.'

'The neighbours were freaking out,' quips Jackie. 'I mean, those poor people were living an ordinary life and suddenly the Troubles land on their street. I've lived in England. There's a genuine fear about what's going on in the North, but people feel cosy because it doesn't affect them. Next thing, you have all these families living close by you. And then, of course, what do you know but Gina is portraying herself as a "victim", asking the housing people there for a council house, after she had put out so many people from their homes on the Shankill.'

Gina was refused a council house on the grounds that 'they

were not suitable tenants because of the potential threat to life'. 'She actually had the balls to go to a homeless charity and get free legal aid to bring Bolton Council to court,' says Jackie. 'She must have been the only homeless person in Britain with £70,000 in her pocket. And then when it did go to court in August, she maintained she didn't know any of the people that had fled with her. Now that's loyalty for you! There were stories about them selling drugs and all sorts "to survive", but they already had plenty of cash. That has come to light since. By Christmas that year both she and Jonathan were charged with conspiracy to supply heroin, cocaine and crack. I mean, it's actually unbelievable.'

The year was also a turning point for Jackie as she was still recovering from 'telling her story' of the years before. After eight long years of silence, in 2002 she decided to cash in her loyalty chips at the terror casino and come clean in the papers about her affair with Adair. 'I always said I would never speak out against Johnny, but my gut turned when I read in the papers that Gina was pining away without her love, that she had to endure 3,000 nights without Johnny and all this nonsense. My mind snapped. I had gone through so much and decided it was time to tell the truth. There were reams of shit in the papers: "My Johnny is no monster, he reads fairy stories to our children at night and when I sit and listen to him, it brings tears to my eyes." More like horror stories! I rang up the Daily Mirror and asked for the person who wrote the article on Gina. The journalist came on the phone and I told her that I was the "other woman" who had had a relationship with Johnny for eight years. I think at first she thought I was a crank because she had received loads of abusive calls that day after Gina's article appeared, but when I told her that I had photographs and years of letters from Johnny in jail [since destroyed], she wanted to meet me straight away.'

The newspaper sold out when Jackie told her story although it didn't all run smoothly. A friend of hers in the Shankill was taken and interrogated by the UDA when they got wind of the article(s). 'John White rang me calling the shots,' she says. 'There was an echo on the phone so I knew he had me on an intercom system within headquarters. Johnny was out at the time and I knew he was sitting there listening. "What do you want?" I asked him. "How did you get my number?" He asked me was I doing a story about Johnny Adair in a daily paper and that the UDA wanted to know if I had betrayed him. "Wait until I tell ye, John," I said, "You tell that little fat bastard, because I know he's in the room listening, I haven't betrayed him one bit. He has betrayed me. I gave him eight years of loyalty." He was trying to get a word in, but when I lose my temper no one can stop me. I told him I was going to hit the "1471 last call" facility on the phone and report the call to my solicitor as harassment, because I knew they hadn't the intelligence to block the number before dialling. That's exactly what I did. About 20 minutes later the phone rang again and it was White. "Well I'm fucking surprised at you, Jackie Legs," he said, but I didn't let him finish. "Why don't you go fuck yourself and I'll tell you what I'm going to do. I'm going to put the phone down and hit the 1471 again, because you probably haven't the intelligence yet again to withhold the number."

'They got paranoid and started ringing the paper, telling them that I was a stalker and that I had been following Adair around for years and so forth, but they didn't realise I had given the paper photographs of myself and Johnny sitting comfortably on my couch with his baby, and other photos of us out at social events—hardly evidence of stalking. I was no kiss and tell after being snubbed by Johnny like they were trying to make out. This is a man who drove me to the brink of madness for eight long years. The reality was no matter how many times I tried to get away from him, he clung on to me like a demented leech. When I read the story in the paper, "Johnny Adair's Lover Reveals All", I got a shock when I read my own words. It was only then that I realised what I had been through, what my kids had been through, and how crazy it had all been. I turned a corner after that.'

Johnny Adair left Manchester for Troon in late 2005 after complaining vehemently that he had been 'hounded and harassed' by the police to the point where he could no longer lead a normal life. While he maintains he doesn't fear death (the IRA, the INLA, British Intelligence, and now British loyalists, have all tried to kill him, he maintains), many believe he faces only one possible end.

'Make no mistake. On the Shankill and in other Protestant areas of Northern Ireland for a long time Johnny Adair was a god to the ordinary people from old age pensioners to young kids,' says Jackie. 'He was their guardian and their armour at the same time. His life revolved around the IRA coming after him and him going after the IRA. Now he's complaining that he was mentally tortured by the powers that be for years and years, that he was taunted by the security forces and Special Branch and God knows who else, and he just wants to lead a normal life. But he has a film crew following him around and any chance he gets to jump on to a newspaper page, he takes it without a second's thought. He says he has nothing against Catholics, but he still hates the IRA for what they did to his country, and that the war was nothing personal, strictly business. He's full of shit. He believes he defended his community from the IRA for all those years and without him there would be a lot more dead Protestants and so on, but has anyone told him that the play is over and it's time to step off the stage?

'The entire thing still haunts me. People stare when I walk about Belfast; I'm still recognised, still branded as Johnny Adair's bit on the side. He chose his woman and by the looks of it, he chose the wrong one. A man doesn't always get the woman he deserves; he deserves the woman he gets. And yes, he truly broke my heart, but I don't think he "got it". I don't think he understood what true loyalty meant at all. I was more of a loyalist than him. That irony will stay with me until the day I die.'